the art of mosaic

the art of mosaic

contemporary ideas for decorating walls,
floors and accessories in the home and garden

CAROLINE SUTER AND
CELIA GREGORY
special photography by Polly Eltes

aquamarine

This edition is published by Aquamarine, an imprint of Anness Publishing Ltd, Hermes House, 88–89 Blackfriars Road, London SE1 8HA; tel. 020 7401 2077; fax 020 7633 9499

www.aquamarinebooks.com; www.annesspublishing.com

If you like the images in this book and would like to investigate using them for publishing, promotions or advertising, please visit our website www.practicalpictures.com for more information.

UK agent: The Manning Partnership Ltd; tel. 01225 478444; fax 01225 478440; sales@manning-partnership.co.uk
UK distributor: Book Trade Services; tel. 0116 2759086; fax 0116 2759090; uksales@booktradeservices.com; exportsales@booktradeservices.com
North American agent/distributor: National Book Network; tel. 301 459 3366; fax 301 429 5746; www.nbnbooks.com
Australian agent/distributor: Pan Macmillan Australia; tel. 1300 135 113; fax 1300 135 103; customer.service@macmillan.com.au
New Zealand agent/distributor: David Bateman Ltd; tel. (09) 415 7664; fax (09) 415 8892

Publisher **Joanna Lorenz**
Managing Editor **Judith Simons**
Senior Editor **Doreen Palamartschuk**
Design Manager **Clare Reynolds**
Designer **Lisa Tai**
Photographer **Polly Eltes**
Photographer's Assistants **Penny Cottee /Ian Tatton**
Stylist **Abigail Aherne**
Indexer **Helen Snaith**
Editorial Reader **Jonathan Marshall**
Production Controller **Claire Rae**

ETHICAL TRADING POLICY
Because of our ongoing ecological investment programme, you, as our customer, can have the pleasure and reassurance of knowing that a tree is being cultivated on your behalf to naturally replace the materials used to make the book you are holding. For further information about this scheme, go to www.annesspublishing.com/trees

Publisher's note
The authors and the publisher have made every effort to ensure that all the instructions contained in this book are accurate and that the safest methods are recommended. Readers should follow all recommended safety procedures and wear protective goggles, gloves and clothing at all times during the making of mosaics. You should know how to use all your tools and equipment safely and make sure you are confident about what you are doing.

The publisher and author cannot accept liability for any resulting injury, damage or loss to persons or property as a result of using any equipment in this book or carrying out any of the projects.

contents

introduction 6

mosaic in history 8

mosaic materials 20

sources of inspiration 30

designing with mosaic 44

walls and floors 64

furniture and ornament 98

sculptural mosaics 124

mosaic techniques 140

mosaic suppliers and artists 156

index 158

acknowledgements 160

introduction

above *Alchemy*: a circular mirror, 400mm (16in) in diameter, made with vitreous glass including bronze-veined mosaic tiles, gold leaf mosaic and acrylic beads, by Claire Stewart.

opposite *Fish and Chips*: information flows along the circuits in microchips the way the eye travels along the individual tesserae in the *andamento* or flow of the tiles. Made of glass, gold, china, ceramic, chrome rope and ancient Venetian glass, by Norma Vondee.

Making mosaics and creating beautiful objects for the home and garden is a hugely creative and enjoyable experience. The materials themselves are exquisite: varied in colour, texture and opacity, and tactile and satisfying to handle.

Mosaic will enable you to add splashes of vibrant, long-lasting colour to the interior and exterior of your home, and perhaps to create pieces to give as gifts to family and friends. These will be truly unique as no two mosaics anywhere in the world, whether or not they are made by the same person, are identical. Each and every one shows the imagination of the person who made it and has its own character and style.

Through the ages, many different cultures all around the world have practised the art of making mosaics and there is a vast range of sources to draw on for inspiration. Some of the background and history of mosaic is discussed here as well as the different styles of mosaic that have evolved. The main considerations to take into account when designing your own mosaics are outlined and the main techniques of mosaic, using the direct and indirect methods, are also demonstrated with instructions on how to assemble your work into a finished piece. There are also a number of different projects suitable for indoors and out for you to work on.

One of the many virtues of mosaic is its flexibility: with so many styles to choose from, you have numerous options. You can work within one particular genre, or you can take elements of various styles and fuse them together, adapting a design to your own specifications. Design is simultaneously the challenge and pleasure of mosaic.

The combination of materials and colours that you opt for will be a purely personal choice. You can assemble them in your own style, using traditional methods as a guide, or you can devise something completely new that no one has done before.

A wealth of materials is at your disposal, from the simplest pebbles to the most complex array of mixed media, such as smalti, marble, vitreous glass, beads, ceramic tiles and mirror. These elements can be formed into a pattern that is either simple or complex, from a geometric border to a full-blown depiction of a landscape or group of people or animals.

You should consider certain basic requirements before starting your mosaic, such as where the piece is to be situated or whether it should be water-resistant, to make sure the mosaic suits the purpose for which it is intended.

Any surface, horizontal or vertical, can be made more beautiful with the addition of mosaic, whether in the form of a panel or covering the whole surface. Indoors or out, walls, floors, ceilings and garden buildings can be given extra impact with the rich jewel shades of multicoloured tesserae. You may decide to make a simple

"No two mosaics anywhere in the world are identical."

rectangular panel of stripes or checks or a realistic or abstract portrait or three-dimensional sculpture. Mosaic lends itself to items as small as a brooch or other pieces of jewellery to a full-size figure or a design that covers an entire floor or wall. Mosaics are absorbing and fulfilling and you are in control of the process from beginning to end, from design to grouting. You will find that you need to concentrate on what you are working on, with few distractions. However, the time spent executing your mosaic designs should be relaxing and the end result will be an attractive and personalized piece of work.

mosaic in history

classical mosaic

Mosaics are an ancient form of art, a skill with pedigree. People have been creating mosaics for thousands of years. The earliest examples we know of come from Sumeria in the Middle East and consist of cones of clay, some plain, some coloured, stuck into wet earth or mud, which then dried and set firm. The ancient Greeks made them too, for example, pebble mosaics from Pella in Macedonia date from the 4th century BC, although the oldest mosaics that most of us are familiar with are probably Roman.

below left The Triumph of Neptune: a typical figurative Roman mosaic depicting a mythological subject with border at Sousse, Tunisia.

below right The Lovers: a detailed Roman mosaic with highly stylized patterns at Piazza Armerina, Sicily, Italy.

The Romans inherited the craft of mosaic from the Greeks and developed it beyond simply making use of pebbles or pieces of stone. They devised the small, specially made tiles (called tesserae) that form the basis of mosaic to this day. Produced in places as far apart as present-day Alexandria and Iraq, the tiles came in a modest range (by today's standards) of natural and earth colours. With them, Roman craftsmen could create beautiful images of birds, animals and mythological monsters, gods and goddesses, men hunting and even girls in bikinis.

As their empire spread, so the Romans exported mosaics abroad. Mosaic was used to decorate buildings around the Mediterranean and beyond, from what is now called Iraq, through Egypt and North Africa, and back round to Italy and Sicily.

walls and floors

The classical style in mosaics generally refers to the designs seen in villas and municipal buildings left to us from the days of ancient Rome and its Empire. Although any remains you may happen to

have visited seem like faded collections of rubble and stones, in their original settings Roman mosaics would have been bright and colourful. Houses, at least those of affluent people such as merchants and businessmen, would have had both walls and floors decorated as lavishly as the owner could afford, in particular any rooms where visitors would have been received or entertained. Floors were decorated with mosaics, walls with frescoes, and the reason that more mosaics than frescoes have survived is because the debris of collapsed buildings sometimes helped to preserve the floor.

representational mosaics

Classical mosaics depict their subject matter in naturalistic terms, a little like a photograph; the aim is to present an image that looks like what it is meant to be. So there are Roman men and women, often in what are clear likenesses of once-living people; there are also dogs, cats, mice, birds and many other animals. The scenes are both domestic and large scale: mosaics show people eating and drinking, the fish that are about to be cooked for their supper and the grapes that will make the wine.

Many Roman mosaics show public life: philosophers disputing, actors preparing to go on stage, soldiers in battle, ships crossing the sea. They tell stories about life at the time and show the wonders of the Roman world: exotic North African landscapes, for example, with their flora and fauna, which formed such a prized part of the Roman Empire.

Mythological subjects, such as the god of the sea, Neptune, are often depicted, especially in harbour or port areas such as at Ostia, Italy.

A typical Roman mosaic appears to us rather like a traditional painting, with a large central section in which the scene is depicted, surrounded by a frame. This frequently takes the shape of a highly

above Images of Neptune and mermen in a monochromatic mosaic at the port of Ostia, Antica, Italy. Sea mythology and marine life are common classical subjects.

decorative border selected from a range of motifs, such as scrolls, meander, Greek key, waves or cubic geometric shapes, or a combination of many of these forms.

byzantine mosaic

Art, and especially mosaic, flourished between the 5th and the 13th centuries, when Byzantium (later renamed Constantinople after the Emperor Constantine, or modern-day Istanbul) was the centre of the Christian world. Whereas the Roman art that has survived to our day is as much secular as religious in its content, the art of Byzantium that has come down to us is almost exclusively religious, and this had an enormous influence on the mosaics of this period.

Byzantine mosaics are beautiful and awe-inspiring. In a turbulent period in history, when the danger of invasion by hostile hordes was all too real, art sent out messages of strength and power. So the strongest impressions made upon us come from the formality, richness and grandeur.

right The Virgin Mary and Christ, in the cathedral of Santa Maria Assunta, Torcello. Formalized poses of religious icons and a lavish use of rich colours such as blue and gold, are characteristic of Byzantine art.

opposite
Elaborate Byzantine architecture with every surface covered in detailed mosaics at the Church of La Martorana in Palermo, Sicily. The desired effect is overwhelming and awe-inspiring.

The figures that appear are for the most part divine. As such, they are intended to inspire devotion (rather than love) through their perfection. Impassive and somewhat remote, they can be vast, dwarfing the human spectator. They are formal as well as formalized, stiff and unbending, their hands raised or spread in a small range of symbolic gestures.

The glory of God demands the best of materials, so Byzantine art is lavish in its use of rich, pure colours, notably reds, blues and greens and, above all, in its use of gold. The mosaics cover almost every surface of a church or basilica – not only ceilings and walls, but also domes and apses. Curved surfaces in particular create dramatic effects when metallics such as gold are lit by flickering candlelight. Even with dim, flat electric light, many a Byzantine mosaic seems on fire with gold.

The scale is often large, covering huge expanses of basilicas, echoing with the sounds of worshippers or enthralled tourists. Such scale makes intimacy impossible, but we can learn from the impact created by richly glowing colours and by the use of metallics, and we can see how stylization creates impact through its simplicity. These striking mosaic effects can be used as inspiration for designs in our homes.

islamic mosaic

The flowing beauty of Islamic mosaics distinguishes them from other styles. Elegant calligraphic forms are an important element, as are geometric or plant-inspired patterns, linked to give an impression of unending repetition. The fluidity and reiteration of the mosaic designs are tasteful and impressive and have a specific aim, which is to encourage the mind of the viewer towards contemplation of the eternal.

The most obvious contrast with Western traditions is that Islamic religious art forbids the representation of the human face or figure, although these do appear in secular or courtly art, in a private context. Instead, any ornamentation for public places, notably religious art, shows intricate geometric patterns, and patterns known as arabesques, which are based on plant (also called vegetal) forms. All these patterns are elaborately intertwined and appear in all manner of colours, from rich reds and blues, to subtle earth tones of saffron and warm yellows, browns, buffs and greens.

above Calligraphy, arabesques and flowing stylized plant forms decorate this mosaic-covered Dubai mosque.

right A highly decorated temple with intricate mosaic work at the Dome of the Rock, Jerusalem.

themes and motifs

Designs tended to be highly stylized, inspired by the natural world and geometry, so while a mosaic might be based on a plant, it does not set out to produce an accurate representation of that plant, but rather to take its essence and weave an intricate pattern from it. The shapes we associate with Islamic mosaics include spirals, lobed designs, stars, leaves and vines, lattices and multi-foil arches, seen in the pierced grilles, shutters and screens that are so typical of this culture. Such designs translate well into mosaic and you can capture the feeling of free-flowing movement in Islamic art in your own work.

The Islamic decorative arts, such as illuminated manuscripts, glassware, textiles and ceramics, were as important as painting or sculpture, and their love of ornamentation was not restricted to items for special occasions. We are familiar with intricately decorated pieces, such as glazed ceramic tiles, intended for everyday use. What is remarkable is the continuity of Islamic artistic traditions, so that art produced in the 10th century may well look like art created recently. And while there are local variations, Islamic art, be it from the Middle East, Moorish Spain or North Africa, retains a strong cultural identity.

latin american mosaic

The Incas, Aztecs, Mayans and other ancient peoples of Central and South America had vibrant, artistic cultures that made beautiful mosaics, which all but vanished after the arrival of the Europeans in the late 15th century. The conquistadors discovered dazzling mosaics in Mexico, such as masks that were worn as symbols of authority and Aztec mosaic headdresses. Modern Mexican mosaics are now well known.

The ornate relics of the Aztecs were encrusted with gold, mother-of-pearl, shells and precious stones, as well as tiny coloured tesserae. The few pieces of pre-Columbian art that survived the conquistadors reveal civilizations that thought on a grand scale. Carved stones or monuments show huge, formalized human figures with elaborate headdresses, surrounded by designs of mythical creatures, monsters and all manner of emblems. This grand scale of work continues in modern mosaic murals.

above An Aztec mythological serpent decorated with turquoise, a much-valued material.

right A detail of a comedian from a mosaic of the History of the Theatre in Mexico at the Teatro Insurgentes, Mexico, by Diego Rivera, 1953.

colours and design

Aztec or Mayan designs are intricate, bold and bright and found in the colours of the most frequently used materials: black from obsidian, gold leaf and turquoise, with perhaps the addition of a rich earthy red, clear green or yellow ochre.

The area was rich in minerals: gold, obsidian, jade and turquoise were worked into jewellery, headdresses and masks, among other objects. The Aztecs used mosaic to cover masks as part of the representation of their deities, working these materials into the design.

Figures with mask-like faces and other aspects of pre-Columbian art, such as fantastical birdman figures, stylized animals and geometric devices, can also be seen worked into colourful modern mosaics.

art nouveau and gaudí

The Art Nouveau period was an extraordinary artistic movement that spanned the Western world in the late 19th and early 20th centuries. It flourished in North and South America, all over Europe, right into Russia. Mosaic art, which had been declining in popularity for some time, became prevalent. It is during this period that Antoni Gaudí developed his unique style of mosaic, decorating many buildings in Barcelona.

The roots of Art Nouveau stem from a variety of stylistic movements, such as the flowing mid-18th-century Rococo style, the Arts and Crafts and Aestheticism movements and the craze for all things Japanese that swept Europe in the 1870s and 1880s. Its origins also lie in a distaste for the mechanization of life, although Art Nouveau's popular appeal was only achieved when mass-production brought furniture, textiles, wallpapers, ceramics and metalwork inspired by the movement within the price range of most ordinary people.

Art Nouveau themes and motifs

The idea behind the movement was to move away from the straight lines and right angles of machine-made objects. Instead, artists sought to reproduce the gentle curves of natural forms, from the twining tendrils of plants to the contours of the human body. So Art Nouveau designs are soft and sinuous, swirling and intertwining, weaving their way across everything from exquisite pieces of jewellery, to chairs, tables and desks.

left Steps, balustrades and benches are covered in mosaic and make an impressive entrance to Gaudí's Parc Güell, Barcelona, Spain.

colours representative of fish scales. Gaudí's rooflines are like no one else's, rising and falling like waves in the sea (yet, for all their fantastical appearance, they are said to be practical, throwing off rainwater with ease and efficiency). High up here too, out of most people's sight, Gaudí indulged his passion for mosaic, covering every undulation and every chimneypot, even the finials at the apex of the still unfinished Sagrada Familia church, to create surreal landscapes that shimmer and glimmer in the light.

left Organic shapes and mosaic walls and roofs characterize Gaudí's architecture in the Casa Battló, 1904–6, Barcelona, Spain.

below A Louis Comfort Tiffany mosaic of two sulphur crested cockatoos.

In cities such as Prague and Vienna, Art Nouveau designs work their way up and around entire buildings, windows, balconies and stair rails. The style often found its way into mosaic. In Belgium, Victor Horta used the medium to decorate the façades of many buildings.

Outstanding among practitioners of the movement are two artists whose creations were the products of truly unique minds. In America, Louis Comfort Tiffany's workshop produced a dazzling range of artefacts. These include the trade-mark lamps most of us are familiar with, and some beautiful mosaics for wealthy New York clients. The mosaics often have a shimmering quality and are of iridescent mother-of-pearl or transparent glass. This might be backed by gold or metal leaf to throw light back to the viewer. Tiffany also added mosaic to large panels and to smaller objects such as trays, inkstands and the bases of his famous lamps.

Antoni Gaudí

The architect Antoni Gaudí (1852–1926) worked around Barcelona and Catalunya at the end of the 19th century in a style known in Spain as *modernista*. His eccentric, reclusive mind produced some of the most extraordinary buildings of the time. The city is still decorated by his work. Not content with sinuously curving balconies, roofs and stairs, entire buildings designed by Gaudí appear to grow organically from the pavements. And, in a fusion of Moorish and contemporary influences, he used mosaic lavishly. The benches in his Parc Güell weave and curve in dizzying, serpentine shapes, and are also covered in Moorish-inspired mosaics that make heavy use of broken ceramics, many in classic blue and white designs.

Gaudí covered entire buildings in mosaic, too. The Casa Battló, for example, is typical in having a façade liberally ornamented with mosaic in

contemporary mosaic

Modern mosaicists work in all manner of styles and bring immense flair to the art. Some draw on traditional influences and methods, others forge new ground in their use of size, shape and materials. In Italy, mosaic remains a vibrant mode of expression. A workshop still thrives in Ravenna, which was the centre of the craft in Byzantine times, and Italy continues to be the main producer of smalti.

There has been a renewed interest in mosaic amongst the general public, and it is notable how mosaic is now being applied to all kinds of objects, in the decorative arts and sculpture, for private enjoyment, and to decorate public places. You can see the effectiveness of mosaic as a hard-wearing design element in locations as varied as railway stations, pools, bars and shopping malls, and many use it to decorate their own homes and gardens.

Mosaic artists all around the world derive inspiration from many sources, including nature, animal and plant forms, as well as from the repeating or geometric patterns typical of Roman, Celtic and Cubist art. The bold and abstract art of 20th-century artists, such as Picasso and Matisse, have also influenced the work of many current mosaic artists. Some employ traditional materials in exciting new ways and others incorporate more unusual materials and textures in their work.

The scale of work varies, from small portable panels and accessories, to patios and large expanses of floor or murals and immense sculptures. One notable example of an giant installation is the work of French artist Niki de Saint Phalle (b.1930). She has created a fabulous mosaic Tarot Garden in Garavicchio, Tuscany, over a period of many years (1979–96) and unites sculpture and mosaic in fantastical figures, using brightly coloured tiles, mirror and glass. Sculptural mosaics are currently popular amongst young artists but there are many prolific mosaic makers who work on panels, murals and indoor pieces.

below left
A fantastical figure in the Tarot Garden, Tuscany, by French mosaic artist Niki de Saint Phalle.

below right A funky, brightly coloured guitar by artist Elizabeth De'Ath.

opposite A pyramid sculpture created with chicken wire and cement by Celia Gregory. The mosaic is made from small pieces of rectangular mirror and stained glass.

mosaic materials

marble, smalti and gold leaf

Mosaic is a versatile art form with great potential for personal creativity. Aside from the enormous design possibilities, the range of materials available is visually exciting, colourful and tactile. As mosaic becomes more popular, the choice of material continues to grow and there are many colour palettes available with varying shades and tones.

above left and middle Marble comes in large slabs that can be cut into squares by hand to produce a more authentic style of mosaic. Machine-cut marble in regular squares on mesh or paper backing are effective for covering large areas.

above right Smalti has been made for over 2,000 years. It is opaque and creates a wonderfully textural finish to your work.

Each mosaic material has its own qualities that will influence the colour, style, look and texture of the finished piece. You can choose to work in just one medium or mix materials to create interesting texture and variety.

marble

This is a natural material; it was used in Graeco-Roman times and is still associated with the luxurious qualities of the modern Italian mosaics. The colours are soft and the variations in tone are subtle: white, chalky pinks and rose, through to delicate greens, blues and blacks. When marble is cut, it has a crystalline appearance and the grains vary according to what part of the world the stone has come from. It is possible to intensify these colours by polishing the marble.

Stone is a hard and durable material. It is excellent for use on floors. For use in mosaics marble is generally cut from rods with a hammer and hardie. It is an expensive material, and this limits its use to the finest quality of mosaic.

You can buy marble that has been machine-cut into regular squares. These squares are laid on to paper backing, which can be removed with water. The handmade characteristic of the mosaic is lost, but it is cheaper and large areas can be covered quickly and easily. The quality of the material is not impaired. Marble is a subtle material: it represents sheer beauty and natural elegance, and has a depth and timeless quality beyond any other material.

smalti

Traditionally made in Italy, smalti is opaque glass and is available in a great variety of colours. Each round slab is made from molten glass fired with oxides, metals and powdered marble and is called a *pizze*. It is individually made and the thickness, colour and size vary slightly each time. Once cooled by a controlled process called annealing, these slabs are cut into tesserae. It is often sold by the half kilo (1¼lb). *Smalti filati* are threads of glass rods of smalti used for micromosaics.

Designs made from smalti have a slight uneven characteristic that creates a brilliant reflective surface. This bumpiness means that smalti mosaics are not often

grouted and cannot be used on floors. Smalti comes in a superb range of colours and any irregularities create character.

gold leaf tile

Always a symbol of wealth, gold is the most opulent tile available to the mosaic artist. Abundantly used in the Byzantine period, it is expensive, yet irresistible, and nothing can surpass its reflective quality. It can be used sparsely in a mosaic and still

above Storing tiles in glass jars is a colourful, practical way to see what you have in stock.

left A selection of tiles with gold and silver leaf, twinkling with luxury and magic.

have a great impact and effect. The tesserae have a backing glass, which is usually turquoise, yellow or green. Then there is a layer of 24-carat gold leaf. It is then protected with a thin layer of clear or coloured glass called the *cartellina*. The gold tesserae can have either a smooth or bumpy surface.

Different variations are available with silver or copper leaf, a thin film of gold alloy or other metals. The colours of tile range from deepest gold to vivid blues and greens. The colours are formed when the *cartellina* or backing glass is altered. The unusual colours need to be ordered from specialist suppliers.

glass and ceramic tiles

These are usually made from vitreous glass and glazed and unglazed clay or porcelain, and come in small regular tiles. They are laid on to mesh or brown paper to make up sheets measuring approximately 30 x 30cm (12 x 12in), which can be used to cover large areas without the tiles having to be laid individually. The range of materials is always expanding and there is a huge variety of colours and shapes to choose from.

glass tiles

Vitreous glass is the most commonly used mosaic glass. It has been standardized and is therefore cheaper than smalti and more accessible to the amateur. It comes in sheets and the individual tile is a regular square about 2 x 2cm (¾ x ¾in). The sheets can be used whole to cover large areas or split down for individual mosaics.

Glass is available in a wide variety of colours. The famous Bizzaria range has a grainy quality to the glass and offers a beautiful selection of tiles that have copper blended into the glass, creating a reflective quality that the other tiles can lack. Cutting the individual tiles into four creates the classic square tesserae; the glass is easy to clip and offers extensive potential for intricate design.

There is a now also a new range of glass mosaic made in France. The colours are more rustic than Bizzaria. The glass is smooth and the concentration of the colour is even throughout, appearing like plastic. When these glass tiles are blended with the other ranges, this gives you a beautiful palette.

Glass is liable to chip or crack so tile manufacturers have developed several types of sheet mosaic that are suitable for floors, which are non-slip and non-absorbent and meet many of the regulations associated with commercial properties. Glass tiles can be shiny, round, square, bumpy, thick, thin, smooth or textured, and come in many different colours. Tiles for mosaic artists are like sweets for children; it is difficult to know which ones to choose. Stored in clear glass jars, the array can be quite spectacular.

ceramic tiles

Mosaic ceramic tesserae are round or square and are made from porcelain. They are good for creating texture as they can be glazed or unglazed. The colour is uniform in unglazed tiles. Ceramic tiles are inexpensive and easily available.

below left **Vitreous glass is a commonly used material; there is a lovely selection of colours. They are easy to clip with mosaic tile nippers.**

below right **Ceramic mosaic tiles come in many shapes and colours, and different kinds of textures.**

above Vitreous glass tiles come on sheets of mesh or brown paper, which are soaked off in warm water. The individual tiles can be clipped into smaller squares.

above Display your mosaic tesserae in groups of colours in clear glass jars. You can easily see what you have available to use, and the gradations of tone and shade.

glass

china, mirror and glass

All the materials mentioned so far mainly build an image using squares. Broken up household tiles build up a mosaic picture in a very different way and offer a whole new world of materials and style. You can buy them new or use tiles you already have with the backing plaster removed. Ceramic tiles are a creative medium in themselves, with beautiful coloured and textured glazes, patterns and images.

below left and right
Plain household tiles are easy and cheap to obtain and can be easily cut to shape. They are good for sculptures and can be useful when you require the mosaic to be water-resistant.

Glazes on household tiles can be shiny and enable you to play with the reflection of light in the design. When smashed up into irregular shapes, they are fantastic for working abstract designs. The random shape of the pieces also makes them excellent for covering three-dimensional and sculptured surfaces. They are easy to handle and allow a freedom in expression that some regular square tiles lack, especially when working over curves.

Household tiles can reflect the contemporary aspect of mosaic, they offer enormous variety and versatility to the mosaic artist and it is possible to cover large areas cheaply.

china

The use of broken china is a wonderful way to recycle and make something beautiful out of otherwise useless items. China is also immensely satisfying to smash. The curving nature of the material gives the final mosaic a textured finish. It is fun buying odd pieces of pottery with quirky handles, lids and patterns. They bring a sense of humour into a mosaic.

A mosaic created with broken china is completely individual because no two pieces of china are likely to be the same. China and crockery are not really suitable for intricate design but are wonderful for working with patterns and texture.

mirror

You can buy mirror in sheets made up of small squares, or rectangles, or in large sheets that need to be smashed up. Mirror works very well scattered through a coloured mosaic; it also produces a fantastic effect when covering entire surfaces. The reflection of light on a sculptured form is spectacular – just think of that mirror ball in a nightclub! The nature of mirror and its reflective quality

means that it constantly changes with the environment. Mirror has a similar magical quality to gold yet you can generally get offcuts from a glazier for free.

stained glass

Walking into a stained glass supplier is like walking into Aladdin's Cave. Not only is there the most beautiful array of colours, but the glass has a wonderful shimmering quality to it, rather like beautiful jewels. There is even a stained glass that is iridescent and reflects light like mother-of-pearl. Some types of stained glass are pieces of art in themselves. They can be used to cover whole surfaces for a luxurious finish or used in small details to highlight details in a picture or an abstract pattern. Use stained glass in your mosaic design when you want to create something extra special.

left Recycling broken crockery to use in mosaic is an inventive and cheap source of materials.

below left Broken crockery can bring humour and variety to mosaics. The uneven quality of cups and plates creates texture, and the patterns and designs are also interesting to play around with in your own designs.

below middle and right Stained glass offers a beautiful array of colours and textures, which possess wonderful reflective qualities. Each sheet of glass could be a piece of art in itself, and when it is broken up into small fragments provides a fantastic mosaic material.

mixed media

In making decorative mosaics, you can use both traditional materials and more unusual found and collected objects, ranging from shells and washed glass collected from beaches while on holiday, to glass jewels, semi-precious stones or glass beads. There are no boundaries and it can be challenging to experiment with new methods and new materials.

below left **Pebbles** are good for creating simple, lasting designs and have natural muted tones and textural qualities.

below middle **Shells** come in beautiful soft colours and are traditionally used in grottoes or garden follies.

below right **Washed glass** and old pottery can often be found on a riverbank.

Using a variety of materials can bring personality and originality to mosaic designs. Mixed materials are particularly effective in sculptural mosaics and for creating a variety of textures and depth in two-dimensional work. It is also fun to gather a collection, such as natural materials from beaches or rivers, or old china from second- hand or thrift stores.

pebbles

Some of the earliest mosaics were made from pebbles and there is still a strong tradition in making pebble mosaics in Greece. In Lindos, Rhodes, you can find many pebble doorsteps and pavements.

Pebbles from the sea or rivers can be found in many subtle variations of colour. There is a certain simplicity that is easy on the eye. They are long-lasting and it is possible to seal the pebbles, which makes them appear wet and the colours richer. Pebbles are traditionally used to cover large areas in gardens. The pebbles offer good drainage and the simple designs look good without being overpowering.

shells

Seashells, in their teeming variety of shapes and colours, have provided inspiration for craftspeople for centuries. The Chinese used mother-of-pearl for

far left **Glass beads** with a flat metallic back used for making jewellery are brilliant for bringing a sparkle to a mosaic.

above left **Small** pieces of washed glass can be added to mosaics for effect.

left **Glass, plastic** and antique beads work well in mosaics, adding texture and colour.

below **Cut stone,** marble and slate into small pieces to create natural, subtle yet textural, mosaics.

shells & beads

inlaying. Shells bedded into lime cement line the grottoes of Italian Renaissance gardens and 18th-century European country houses adorned their garden follies with them. They are fun to collect and bring a natural beauty to a mosaic.

salvaged materials

The edges of washed glass and pottery have been smoothed and rounded by years of erosion in the water and can be found on beaches and riverbanks. The effect of the water also softens the colours to create a gentle mosaic material. Collected or salvaged materials could include anything from old coins to forks and spoons. You could build an image up from pieces of aluminium or metal foil, building blocks or perhaps even cover a sculpture in dice.

beads and jewels

Glass beads and jewels catch the light and twinkle. Their unevenness creates texture which emphasizes the detail in a mosaic. Antique beads often have peculiarities within the glass that is distinctive. You can buy jewels that have a flat back, which are easier to lay. Beads and jewels placed in a mosaic add glints of colour and reflections.

sources of inspiration

figurative mosaics

The depiction of the human form can take several guises. It can be realistic, as the Romans chose, or it can be more abstract. The Romans preferred the representational style in their mosaics. As in their other arts, they did not confine themselves to idealization, favouring a realism that was at times quite literally "warts and all". In their sculpture, for instance, even emperors or senators could be shown with thinning hair, furrowed foreheads and bulbous noses.

Figurative mosaic in the hands of an expert may lend itself to great detail and intricacy. In such mosaics, the contours of the face and body are skilfully rendered through the way tesserae are cut to size and positioned for their shape – notably to show the jut of the chin, cheekbones and brow. Tesserae are chosen to suggest the modelling of the features, for their gradations of colour and tone and to show the way light and shade falls on the face or body.

right *Satyr and Maenad*: a highly detailed replication by Salvatore Raeli, of a 2nd-century mosaic panel from the House of the Faun, Pompeii.

In Byzantine times, the depiction of the human form became stylized. As we have seen, mosaic was largely confined to religious or imperial subjects and was concerned to show figures such as emperors, Christ, God, the Virgin Mary and the saints, and for these, idealization was the aim. Forms were made slender, elongated and more elegant, faces became regular and expressionless, gestures and rituals (such as benediction) were formalized and ritualized. It is a style that continues to inspire mosaic artists today.

moving with the times

Mosaics in later centuries, including the Renaissance and Victorian eras, remained largely classical and representational in inspiration. During the 20th century, however, there was a move towards the abstract representation of human figures.

This style of depicting people was practised by many artists, including the superb workmanship of Pablo Picasso, Matisse and Chagall: their styles lend themselves well to mosaic with the emphasis on outline and colour rather than detail, and the free rendition of line and form. Mosaic artists can choose to depict the human form in many ways, varying from ethnic art to the strip cartoon.

far left *Saint Ordalaffo Falier*: coloured and gold leaf smalti and raku-fired pieces by Martin Cheek.

left *Sourire*: a bold, African tribal mask-like face by Stephen Smith.

below A disc jockey mixing his decks is installed on a wall, in a mosaic designed for a musician by Celia Gregory. The square tiles have been laid in straight lines coming out from the centre and expanding into the border, creating a feeling of vibration.

animals, insects and birds

Since prehistoric man scratched the outlines of horses and oxen on cave walls, the animals, insects and birds that surround us have fascinated human beings. They provide an endless source of inspiration in all arts and crafts, not only mosaic. The Romans frequently showed domestic and wild animals in their mosaics.

below left A rabbit panel by Claire Stewart shows the broad outlines of the animal's body.

below right Takako Shimizu's mosaic of a cobweb and spider brilliantly conveys the delicacy and transparency of the web. The soft colours work well on this garden wall.

The ancient Roman images were mostly realistic, though sometimes they conveyed a quirky sense of humour. Animals in art have often served a symbolic purpose, for example, dogs can indicate fidelity. Birds were a common Roman subject, especially doves at a fountain, which suggested harmony and peace.

modern depiction

The current revival of interest in mosaic often displays a more naturalistic approach, revelling in the beauty and detail of the natural world. Nature can be depicted in numerous ways. A bird could be the main focus within a panel or roundel, or be a stand-alone image on a plain background, such as a garden wall.

How the mosaic is executed will depend on the artist's own style: animals and birds can be treated in a symbolic manner, or they can be allegorical or humorous, realistic or naturalistic. They can appear in outline against a one or two-colour background or in silhouette, or have two or three-dimensional effects.

More unusual materials can be added to give detail, texture and depth to the piece.

Often animals, birds and insects will form part of a larger mosaic; when they do there needs be to be enough tonal contrast in the work to allow the images to stand out and colours must be chosen carefully. Birds and insects are challenging subjects, but the potential for using vibrant colour is endless, especially in bright plumage.

above Nature in the raw: a tigress snarls in this Roman mosaic, which is full of life and movement.

right Takako Shimizu's well-camouflaged mosaic bat has texture and a three-dimensional quality.

far right A detailed pebble mosaic bird by Maggy Howarth demonstrates the skill, intricacy and subtlety that can be achieved by using different pebble shapes, colours and tones.

marine life

The ocean and the teeming variety of life found in it have provided the mosaic artist with a rich source of inspiration for centuries. Mosaic work is frequently used near water or to contain it, such as on bathroom walls and floors, in swimming pools, or externally on fountains and water features. Marine life is therefore an appropriate subject for the artist to use when creating decorative schemes.

Mosaic materials, especially the intense and vibrant material smalti, suit the beautiful colours of fish and the many shades of the ocean, such as emerald, azure, turquoise and aquamarine. Such themes offer wonderful opportunities for mosaic artists to experiment with exciting and vivid colour.

Marine life, such as fish, dolphins, octopus, starfish and seaweed, can create a flowing mosaic design, full of action and energy. The impression of water, light and movement can be conveyed effectively and with surprising economy in the way the tesserae are laid. Artists can intersperse the mosaic with iridescent and reflective materials, such as mirror, to highlight certain areas and create a glistening scene.

Mosaics of marine life are often very graphic and highly patterned. The scales on fish often look like mosaics themselves, and mosaic artists can depict this with intricate detail.

above **A detail from a picture frame by Norma Vondee, showing a classical-style dolphin.**

right **Roman mosaic provided great inspiration for artists throughout the last millennium. This reproduction, using tiny pieces of marble and stone, depicts sea creatures intended to look as if they are swimming around a classical water feature.**

above *Over the Wave*: a close up of a large triptych inspired by the sea, made from Venetian smalti, gold leaf piastre, slate, granite chippings and marble dust, by Jane Muir.

left A close up of a soft coral smalti mirror frame decorated with sea creatures, by Norma Vondee.

right A detailed and glistening John Dory fish in the sea. Made from smalti and mirror by Martin Cheek.

plants and flowers

Over millennia, human beings have delighted in preserving the fragile beauty of plants and flowers through art, be it as paintings, drawings, sculptures, in gold or silver, in enamel or glass – or mosaic. The natural world, especially plants and flowers, are appealing subjects for the mosaic maker. Plants and flowers soothe the senses, are easy on the eye to look at, their beauty is constant and they can be depicted in many different styles.

Natural plant forms are a very popular theme in mosaic. Often plants are woven into the designs of mosaic borders. They can flow around a panel or large mural creating wonderful rhythm and activity that adds interest and depth to a design. Plant forms can be depicted in a very elegant and stylized manner.

Contemporary mosaicists often use the medium's graphic qualities to produce outstanding work based on natural forms. Bold colours and chunky textures can combine to create vivid three-dimensional images. Plants and flowers are also excellent individual images, perhaps for table tops and panels, as the petals, leaves and stems lend themselves well to flowing ornamentation. Trees, especially the tree of life, are a common theme in mosaic.

The images could be depicted in subtle materials, such as marble, and have delicate, soft-toned flowers, or they could be bold and graphic and less representational, using funkier colours and materials such as vitreous glass and mirror. Ceramic tiles can give a warm, earthy feel to mosaic pictures of plants.

left *Tree of Life*: a panel with a border of hand-painted Mexican tiles by Helen Baird. Trees are a popular source of inspiration in mosaic.

top The knobbly textured surface of a pineapple vividly conveyed by Norma Vondee.

above This garden ornament by Rebecca Newnham shows how well natural plant forms can be expressed abstractly.

above Detail of part of the bush from *Bird on a Bush*: a marble mosaic using soft, warm tones, by Salvatore Raeli.

nature

landscapes and still life

Entire landscapes have been depicted in mosaic – even, in one example at the abandoned Roman port of Ostia, a surprisingly accurate map of the world.

To accompany their idealized figures, the Byzantines depicted equally stylized landscapes of green grass, docile sheep and wild flowers, or rich blue night sky-scapes, against which gold stars glisten. To show an entire landscape in mosaic – to produce complex images of the undulations of hills and valleys, the gradations of blue sky or the reflection of water – requires great skill, time and patience.

As with any painting, the creation of a landscape begins with the composition. It needs to be planned and sketched out, and the order of work and colours and tones of the tesserae need to be considered in advance.

Landscapes can, at first glance, appear to be faithful to reality, but most involve a certain amount of stylization, of tidying up, of selecting particular subjects for the foreground and background, of high-lighting details and trying to create a feeling of distance and three-dimensional space. Images are built up by laying lines of regular or cut tesserae around images such as trees or hills, and backgrounds can include many other patterns. A mosaic landscape is like a pixellated image that has to be viewed from a certain distance for it to come into focus.

Mosaic landscapes in earlier centuries were often very detailed like paintings, but images do not have to be naturalistic to be effective. Some contemporary mosaic artists take inspiration from naive art and the surreal landscapes of De Chirico, and they have produced scenes that make full use of mosaic's textural and graphic qualities. They suggest a complete landscape rather than showing highly detailed images and objects.

still lifes

The portrayal of "inanimate" or lifeless objects, such as flowers, wine or food destined for the table is a popular mosaic theme. Care needs to be taken when combining elements of the image, placing them within the picture area and outlining them to make a striking design. Neutral backgrounds work well with vivid foreground images.

below This highly skilled mosaic from the period of Imperial Rome depicts people fleeing the power of the Nile in flood. All sorts of incidents are crammed into an impossibly small space in order to relate the story.

top *Candlesticks and Fruit*: this still life by Rosalind Wates is all about contrast. The *opus regulatum* effect of regular, square tiles in straight rows provides a static setting.

above A detailed landscape using minute tesserae, almost like micromosaic.

left *Environment*: a landscape by Stephen Smith using both randomly and uniformly-placed tiles.

geometric and abstract

Many mosaics make use of non-representational geometric and abstract patterns of one form or another. The range of motifs is almost limitless, and can include cubes, checks and chequerboard, ropes, interlocking squares or circles, herringbone, basketweave, spirals and triangles. Geometric patterns that form repeated designs are ideal for mosaic borders.

below left Blue and turquoise tiles are laid in a geometric pattern set diagonally to the surrounding patio. Patterns in ponds are best kept simple.

below right Patchwork mosaic is reflected in the sides of this sunken pond feature.

opposite Echoes of the art of Paul Klee are visible in this geometric bird bath. The grid effect is offset by the changes in colour.

By their nature, geometric patterns are very well suited to the art of mosaic. The basic outline is simple and ideal for the shape of tesserae, but shapes can be repeated as often as is needed. The repetition is not monotonous; quite the opposite. The effect can be soothing and pleasing to the eye, and variations can be achieved through different colourways.

pattern

A repeated pattern is an effective way of linking spaces: for instance, a path and hallway could both be in a simple chequerboard pattern, the path in, say, black and white, and the hall in blue and white. The transition from outdoors to indoors is conveyed by the change in colourway. And where the two areas are relatively small, keeping the pattern the same makes the overall space seem larger by providing continuity.

There are many standard geometric patterns to choose from, such as the Greek key, which remains ever-popular, or the intertwining, flowing rope designs of Celtic art, or Islamic or Arabic sinuous calligraphic motifs. Geometric shapes frequently occur in 20th-century art and the blocks of colour of, for example, Mondrian would translate well into a mosaic project.

designing with mosaic

considerations

The wide choice of materials available means that designing a mosaic is a highly personal process. Your mosaic can be any size from a pair of earrings or a brooch, to a chair, table or water feature, or a complete floor or mural. You can be inspired by an existing design or devise one that is totally original. Your choice of image or pattern can also connect the design directly to its maker or to its recipient.

above **Square tesserae** are the basis of most mosaic work and can be laid whole or clipped to the desired shape and laid in a variety of ways.

right **Mosaic** is an ideal medium for bathrooms. Using the same stone on floors, walls and bath surround gives a sophisticated and unified look. Sicilian mosaic limestone tiles are used here.

When you are designing with mosaic, you have the liberty to use just one material, such as smalti, or combine as many as you wish. Sometimes, this freedom can make it harder to reach decisions. But, of course, no object exists in a vacuum and there will other factors to consider when creating your designs. Your mosaic may be intended for a predetermined place within a room or open-air space, where other objects may surround it. It may also be used for a specific purpose, such as to contain water. Your designs should also take into account that mosaic is long-lasting and the colours virtually permanent. Unlike textile, paper or even paint, stone, glass and ceramic do not disintegrate; they do not break easily or fade. Once the setting medium is hard, changes cannot be made. These qualities are the great strengths of mosaic, but they mean you cannot go over your work and cover it up.

Do not worry; all you need to do is be clear in what you want to achieve and how you want to realise it. Do this, and materials, colour and style will marry happily with setting, mood and size and you will have a mosaic you are proud of. But before committing tesserae to adhesive, consider the following points.

function

Always consider the function of the mosaic. Is it to be practical or decorative? Because most mosaic is hardwearing and water-resistant, it is quite safe to use for items such as splashbacks behind the bathroom or kitchen sink, or for the floor of a hallway, garden room or patio. If the work is to withstand wear and tear from feet or soap and water, think about which

materials will be best suited to your needs: glass, for example, is not so suitable for the passage of feet, bikes and perhaps the odd piece of garden equipment. However, if a purely decorative effect is what you are after, clearly these considerations do not apply and your choice is wider.

location

Consider where the mosaic is to be positioned. Every aspect of the design – whether it is simple or complex, abstract or representational, the size, the colours to be used, and the materials – is influenced by which room of the house the mosaic is intended for, or its position in the garden.

focal point

Decide whether the mosaic is to stand out from or blend in with its surroundings. Will it be the focal point of a decorative or planting scheme, or is it to go with established furniture or features? Your answers will determine how strong the design needs to be.

mood

Consider the impact and mood the mosaic is to create. It is worth being clear at an early stage just how much of a centrepiece you want your mosaic to be, as it is a strong medium that can easily upstage its surroundings. The mosaic can be as bold as you like, but its style should have a link with its situation. A bright geometric mirror frame will jar in a guest bedroom that is decorated in soft florals; likewise a large panel in bright folk art reds and oranges might swamp a tiny but sophisticated all-white courtyard garden.

size

You need to decide the size of the mosaic. Ensure that the design is in scale with the overall size: a tiny pattern will look out of place in a large mural, while a big pattern will look just as wrong in a tiny space. Remember, too, that patterns or designs look larger the closer they are to your eye level. Look at one of the illustrations in this book at eye level, then put the same

above *Fairies*: a beautiful abstract image of three fairies made from mirror and iridescent stained glass by Celia Gregory. The reflective quality of the materials means that the mosaic constantly changes as different light hits the surface.

page on the floor; you will see how much detail is lost. Operate on a "less is more" principle and take out superfluous detail for smaller-scale pieces or those that will only be viewed from afar.

siting your mosaic

When designing a mosaic for an interior or exterior space, there are some important factors to consider. To aid you in your planning and preparation and to help you avoid making time-consuming mistakes, consider the questions in the boxes and be clear about the purpose of your design, taking into consideration if it is a practical or decorative mosaic.

Mosaic is a bold medium and you can cover large areas with it and create dramatic effects. Indoors, especially, it will be a strong feature. You want it to be striking but, if it is large, not to overpower its surroundings. Bear these considerations in mind when beginning to plan work on design, colour and size.

Being so durable, mosaic is ideal for out of doors where wind, rain and frost would quickly see off a less hardwearing medium. When considering your initial design, make sure your mosaic fits in with its environment. Ensure the location of your mosaic is suited to the plants, the surrounding garden features and the house.

right In a restrained modern setting, designed by Marion Lynch, this striking mirror frame is all the ornamentation you need.

opposite left A dull brick wall is enlivened by an impressionistic mosaic of a cockerel by Takako Shimizu.

opposite right The hot colours of this small water feature by Tabby Riley suit the exotic planting around it.

points to consider

- What is the mosaic's function?
- Which room is it going in?
- Is the room's colour scheme being built around the mosaic?
- If not, does the mosaic fit in with the existing scheme?
- Is the design you like appropriate to the room where you intend to place the mosaic?
- Is the weight of the object and the material used appropriate to the function and position?
- What happens if you decide to redecorate your home?
- Is the mosaic portable (wall-mounted for instance, or on furniture)?
- If not, what happens when you later want to move it to another place, or take it with you when you move into different accommodation?

for interiors

light

Bear in mind the nature of daylight where you live, which is essentially blue in temperate areas and more red in tropical parts. Take some tesserae outside to see how natural light alters their colours. There is no reason why you cannot use strong, hot colours in temperate areas, but be aware of how vibrant they can look. Mosaics in brilliant reds and oranges need to be carefully placed in temperate gardens. If allowed to peep from under lavish green planting, however, they can add a touch of drama and humour, and are good for shady areas, dark courtyard gardens or a particular "room" in a large garden, perhaps set among hot-toned flowers. Using cool blues and greens in warmer settings can conversely create an area of calmness and tranquillity.

points to consider for exteriors

- What is the mosaic for?
- Where is it going?
- Do you want it to blend in with established plants and garden features, or is it the centrepiece from which all else flows?
- Are the colours suitable for its purpose, size and location?
- Is the mosaic the right size for its specific purpose (not so small that it is lost, nor so big that it dominates the space)?
- If it is to convey information, such as a house name or number, is the design clear enough and uncluttered with detail to enable it to be viewed from a distance?

siting

Clever positioning is part of a successful mosaic, where all aspects of its design (subject, pattern, framing, colour, texture and size) come together in the right setting. You might like to choose a design that is appropriate for the site, for example food in the kitchen or grapes and vines in the dining room.

When you are working in a room on a ceiling or floor, consider the viewing lines, the entrances and exits, and where the mosaic can be seen from. If the mosaic is to be seen at an angle, make sure it gives the best view. If the piece is in a public or architectural setting, make sure the design works and is sympathetic to the existing surroundings.

Mirrors should be sited adjacent to windows and not opposite, to achieve the best effects. Subtle colours should be positioned with care so the colours are enhanced, not lost by glare or bright light.

scale

The size of your design is important, so bear this in mind when planning and eliminate detail that will be lost at a distance. This applies equally to the actual size of the tesserae you are working with. Choose tiles that will look right for their intended position: the pieces must not be so large that they cannot cope with the design or pattern you want; but neither should they be too small or they will tend to look untidy and ineffective.

using colour

One of the most fundamental elements of any design in any medium is the colour – it has a profound effect on the way we respond to an object. In addition, the way light, real or artificial, falls on these colours is hugely important and is a factor to consider from the very beginning of your project. If using large areas of the same colour, be sure to vary the tone and sizes of the pieces to add interest.

When deciding what colours you want to use, make sure you have some samples to hand and place them in the setting you have in mind. See how the natural light falls on them. The closer to the window they are, the stronger the colours will look. If they are set on a wall between two windows and against the glare of daylight, however quite the opposite happens and they will appear darker. What is more, the same shade of red will look slightly different when placed flat on the floor and when hung vertically on the wall. Also – as anyone who has tried to match colours under fluorescent lighting or caught sight of themselves in the average elevator mirror will know – the light source can profoundly affect some colours. Make sure you look at your colour samples in all the types of light in which they will be seen (daylight, tungsten bulb, halogen, neon and so on), and also consider how the light changes at different times of the day.

hot and cool colours

What we perceive as colourless white light is divided into the colours of the spectrum – red, orange, yellow, green, blue, indigo and violet.

These divide broadly into hot colours (red, orange and yellow) and cold (green, blue and indigo). The shades that centre around violet (a mixture of red and blue) tend to be cooler, depending on the proportion of red to blue: mauve and lilac incline to cool, maroon and purple to warm.

In addition, colours are predominant or recessive: in other words, some catch the eye more than others. It is not just a question of light and dark, but of which colours attract the eye first, and which colours it turns to second. Glance casually at a selection of colour images and try to

below A small indication of the vast range of colours and hues of smalti that are now widely available to the mosaic artist.

above Using darker and lighter colours throws different elements of a design into relief and brings others to prominence.

above A strong colour used against a light background stands out more clearly than white on a coloured background.

above Notice how the use of colour alone produces entirely different results from the same pattern.

notice where your eye instinctively goes first. You will probably find that it alights immediately on any reds, oranges or yellows, or any strong, clear colours (in an all-blue room, for instance, the eye goes first to the brightest shade of blue). Only after that does it move to the more recessive tones, the blues (or softer shades of blue in our all-blue room), the greens and the browns.

So, when deciding what colours you want to use, bear in mind the visual effect they will have. A palette of reds, oranges and yellows will create a warm impression. They will also be strong, dominating their surroundings. And because they

draw the eye, they will make spaces seem smaller. This need not be a disadvantage: an entrance hall in warm tones will seem extra-welcoming on a cold winter's night; a north-facing bathroom can have the chill taken off it and be made to feel small and cosy by decorating with colours from the warm end of the spectrum.

Blues, greens and indigos are cool colours; coupled with the "hard" effect of mosaic, they may make a cold room seem more so. Along with browns they are recessive, so they will be well suited to making small spaces seem larger providing you do not opt for too many dark tones, as these will make areas seem more

confined. So soft blues, greens and lilacs would be a good choice for a mosaic at the end of a small garden.

When it comes to dark and light colours, received wisdom is that a dark area stands out more when surrounded by light-toned colours. This will happen provided the colours are not too bland (too much magnolia, cream or beige can be dull). However, it can often be as successful to play up the dark aspect by choosing a similar tone of another colour. The secret is to make the colour deep but rich: choose dark scarlet red or blue, blackcurrant, peacock blue, racing green or chocolate brown. Boldness pays off.

matching colour to style

Another very important aspect of colour is that the palette you choose must match the style of the design if the whole is not to look incongruous. A folk art pattern would not suit a combination of chrome yellow, black and silver while an Art Deco design would work less well in primary blue, red and yellow. A realistic floral mosaic will be most successful executed in colours as close as possible to the real plant, while a piece inspired by the work of Tiffany asks for his characteristic turquoises, lavenders, chartreuse greens and soft pinkish whites. A marine design would look right in blues, greens and sand.

left Ideas and designs derived from the sea often look best in blues, greens and sandy shades.

below left Decorative mosaics can be used as accessories to co-ordinate with existing schemes and fittings. For example, this mirror frame echoes the coral marble sink unit.

matching colour to existing schemes

You will need to take into consideration the items with which your mosaic will be surrounded; however much you may want it to make a splash, it needs to bear some relation to what is around it, or it will simply look out of place.

Study the furniture, the walls, the curtains and the other fabrics and items in the room. Is there an overall colour scheme? If so, blend your mosaic with it, perhaps picking up on some of the colours in a particular item, such as a display cabinet or a fireplace.

Whether it is to go on the wall, be placed on the floor, or sit on another item, a mosaic panel needs to relate to the wall or floor colour. Perhaps the background colour could be one or two tones lighter or darker than the walls or floors. Perhaps its design could echo the colour of the tiles in a tiled hall; or its frame could replicate other picture frames in the room.

colour

cool and warm light

The fact that the quality of light varies depending on which country you live in becomes particularly relevant when considering the garden. In temperate latitudes, the light, even in midsummer, tends to be blue.

In the Mediterranean and tropical parts of the world, the light is significantly warmer and redder. This explains why the colours of Provence, Italy or Santa Fe in New Mexico (ochres, terracottas and earth tones with splashes of cobalt blues and rust reds) look so right there but do not always translate so well in temperate zones. By contrast, the soft greens, browns and grey-blues that suit cloudy skies can look too subdued and washed out in stronger sunlight.

white and dark grout

In mosaic, the gaps between the pieces are as much a part of the design as the tesserae themselves and these gaps are filled by a grouting medium. The effect of the mosaic varies dramatically depending on the colour of grout chosen: a white grout will make the overall effect very much lighter; a dark grout is deep and sombre but can create contrast. It is well worth testing out a small sample to decide what effect you want.

top The colours of the mosaic tiles have been carefully chosen to echo the vases on the windowsill.

above Decide early on whether you want white or dark grouting as this will affect the overall appearance of the mosaic.

left Soft, rain-washed colours suit temperate gardens and match surroundings well.

using contrast

The element of contrast adds drama and movement to a design, and is necessary to satisfy the eye and keep it interested. At first glance, it may look as though a scheme has avoided any contrast, especially if soft, muted colours are used, but the artist can introduce contrast in many ways. It can be used in the materials selected, the colour, tone and shapes of tesserae, the methods of laying them and the textural surface of the mosaic.

right Within this soft natural colour palette, contrast comes from the juxtaposition of the star with the circle and the unglazed and glazed tiles.

below Shape and colour both give contrast here, as a river of pointed shards flows between a retaining border of square tiles.

In mosaics, you need to create contrast to ensure your design remains attractive and intriguing. It is easily achieved by mixing materials and varying their texture, changing the colours and sizes of the pieces, and by introducing elements of surprise, such as gold or silver, metallics, mirror and deliberately broken or strangely shaped pieces. Experiment with the fall of light and the transparency or opacity of the work.

You can also achieve contrast by making a soft, sinuous, flowing design out of an intrinsically hard material. What are termed mixed media mosaics (where two or more different materials are used) create the vital element of contrast simply through the mixture of materials.

size and shape

One standard method of cutting tesserae is cutting them into quarters; eighths of tiles are often used in a continuous line for outlining shapes. However, mosaic materials can be cut into numerous shapes, including squares, rectangles, triangles, and with practice even semicircles and wedge shapes. Create contrast by varying tile sizes and shapes within patterns and various areas of the design. For example, on a round table top, you could

mosaic a circular central section with large, unstructured broken household tiles and then create contrast with a border around the central part made up of neatly laid tiles in a more formal design, or with distinct shapes, such as diamonds or triangles.

shaping mosaic

Because of their shape, which is often square, and their hard texture, mosaic tesserae are well suited to geometric or angular design. However, there is no reason at all why you cannot deliberately play up the visual differences between

squares of clay or glass and sensuous curves and arcs. Think of Gaudí's extraordinary houses in Barcelona, where the undulating walls and roofs flowing up and down like ocean waves, are covered in gleaming tiles and mosaic.

colour

Using colour is a simple but effective way of providing contrast, perhaps in a mosaic made entirely from one material: an obvious instance would be a floral mosaic in which the flower is brilliantly coloured and the background is plain, perhaps white, palest green, or even pale grey. Using just black and white is the most extreme contrast, or you could limit yourself to one or two dark and light colours to focus on how the tiles are cut and laid, and experiment with patterns in individual areas. If a bright, vibrant look is what is desired you could use combinations such as scarlet with blue or purple with yellow. However, contrasts do not have to be extreme to work; shades of the same colour, or a palette of related tones can be just as effective.

varying materials

A touch of the unexpected is an ideal way of enlivening a design. A matt chequerboard in black and white can be transformed by placing silver or glass tesserae at random intervals. A pebble pool surround may be brought to life with a few beautifully shaped shells. The regularity of a geometric design can be counterpointed by one larger or several smaller areas of irregular broken ceramic pieces. A monochrome mosaic can change

beyond recognition with a panel made of broken patterned china, whether in the same or a contrasting colour. Give free rein to your imagination and experiment.

above The long, curving wall covered in smashed ceramic pieces by Gaudí creates an unexpected seating area in Parc Güell, Barcelona, Spain.

left An elegant alcove created using rectangular stone mosaic by Robert Grace. The side wall contrasts with the other surfaces as the tesserae are laid in a more haphazard manner. The gold mosaic panels are of the *Madonna,* a Byzantine replica, and the *Young Patrician,* both by Salvatore Raeli.

using pattern

You can create almost any pattern or shape you want with mosaic, particularly when you have gained some experience of cutting and working with the medium. Examples from antiquity to the present day show how skilled craftsmen can work enormous detail and varied patterns into their designs. There is a branch of the craft known as micro-mosaic, which uses *smalti filati* and makes even greater detail and pattern possible. These mosaics are very intricate and skilled.

below left This detail from a larger mosaic shows various ways of changing direction and outlining movement.

below middle The lines in this mosaic are laid in curves and give a wonderful sense of movement.

below right Bold, strong patterns can be made by using larger, clipped pieces of tiles.

If you are a beginner, it is sometimes better to consider mosaic a medium that is most effective in broader outline rather than fine detail. Unlike drawing or painting, mosaic may become less effective the more it is weighed down with detail; a few bold outlines can be filled in with patterns and shapes. Pattern alone can be the focus of a mosaic.

simple outlines

If you are a good draughtsman or woman and you do draw or paint, you may find your initial attempts at design may not be quite right for mosaic, as you will be tempted to add too much detail by way of shading, moulding and modelling.

To start with, you may like to study the work of cartoonists that evoke people, places and whole landscapes with a few lines of the pen. See how a facial expression is conveyed with single strokes for eyes, brows, mouth and so on; notice how movement is expressed. Equally, you could examine the cut-outs in the late work of Matisse to see how brilliantly he captured the contours of the human body in movement in pieces of coloured tissue paper. Experiment with this "less is more" principle yourself.

left The simple, but elegant, circular design of these table tops by Rebecca Newnham echoes the shape of the objects and focuses the eye on the luscious material.

below The pattern of the broken china and tiles worked in between the plain white tiles emphasizes the design, which is built up around a few basic outlines and shapes, by Cleo Mussi.

If you prefer to adapt a pre-existing design, then all you need do is trace the basic shape, then hold it away from the original to make sure the outlines are sufficient to show what it is you wish to portray. Next, make your outlines the right size. With modern photocopiers that enlarge or reduce, this is easily done.

forming patterns

The art of laying tesserae to form images and patterns is called *opus* (*opera* is the plural). There are no strict rules to adhere to as each artist develops his or her own style, but there are a few things to consider. A fan shape is frequently seen in mosaic and this gives pattern and interest to a background, especially if you are laying just one colour. Use a pair of compasses to help draw in the curves. Rows of straight square tesserae laid like brickwork can also fill large areas.

When laying circular mosaics, again draw in guidelines with a large pair of compasses. If the design comes to a central point then make angled cuts as you work the centre. This can be fiddly and involve using tiny pieces, however, you could cover the central point with a large piece of tesserae and work around it.

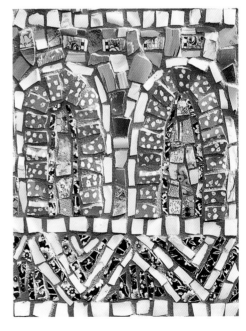

pattern

rhythm and variety

These are essential elements of pattern. When the lines of tesserae flow around a particular subject or group of subjects and create rhythm and movement, it is called *opus vermiculatum*. Images can also be outlined in the background colour or in a distinct colour to help emphasize it and define the shape and pattern. Laying two or three lines of tiles around a shape will also add clarity to the design. Lines of tesserae can be laid to flow in directional lines, leading the eye to or around a design: this is called *andamento*.

To add variety to a mosaic, you could lay random patterns of tiles. Sometimes this is necessary to fill awkward or assymetrical shapes. You can vary the interstices, or spaces between the tesserae, depending on the effect you require.

Geometric shapes are ideal for creating rhythm in mosaics and they will not become monotonous. Squares or oblongs, checks, chevrons, circles, swirls or spirals, Greek key, interlocking or separated –

left **It is possible to create wonderful patterns with square mosaic tesserae. The lines in this mosaic piece are laid in curves that give a great sense of movement.**

below left **Variety abounds, through the use of colour, shape and both reflective and non-reflective materials.**

below right **A brightly patterned and very smoothly polished, Islamic-style marble table top made by Salvatore Raeli.**

all are intrinsically pleasing to the eye and have an inbuilt sense of movement. It is why these motifs have remained so popular across the world.

shading with pattern

Often, you will need to convey some variation in shading and change colour in a mosaic. You may stagger lines of colour in alternate rows to create fingers of colour or introduce some tonal shading so the change is not too abrupt. This often occurs in patterns using subtle colours. Some degree of moulding or shading is vital in representational mosaics, and this can be achieved by varying the size and/or the shape of your mosaic pieces, as well as their colour, to suggest the contours of a face (nose, eyes, chin, brow), the body and limbs, or the shape of a flower. This is a skilled procedure. Be sure to practise carefully beforehand, laying out your pieces like a jigsaw puzzle on a piece of cardboard, well away from any setting medium, until you are sure every piece is in the right place.

Grout lines also play a part in helping the rhythm and flow of a design. Straight lines give a more formal, structured effect and curved lines help give a feeling of movement. The widths and colours of the lines can vary.

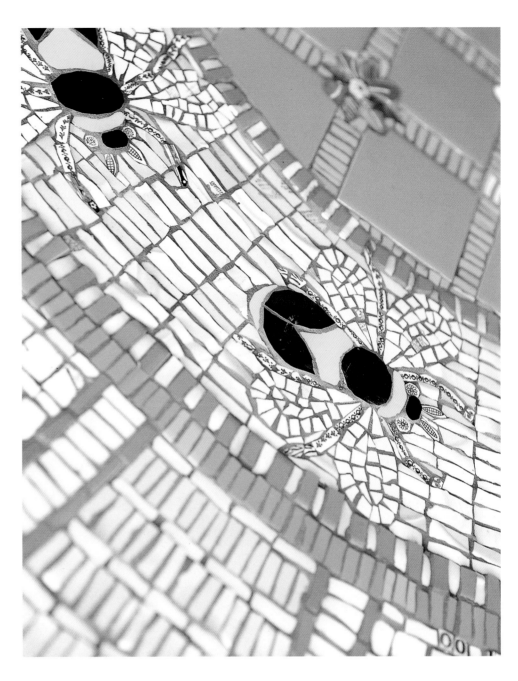

right *Arch Air Condensed*: detail of a bee from a recycled china mosaic by Cleo Mussi. The background patterns are as vivid as the bees.

below Light falls on the eyes and nose, features that are skilfully conveyed through a varied use of pattern and colour.

using texture

Texture can be one of the most interesting, exciting aspects of mosaic. Because it is a three-dimensional and tactile medium, mosaic has depth and character by its very nature. Even if you are working on a flat panel, the depth of smalti, tile or glass can vary and you can introduce many materials to vary the surface of a mosaic and create sparkling shapes and textural schemes.

Different materials have their own inherent qualities. Clay or ceramic are even but have a slight organic roughness. Metal is hard and angular. Wood is rough but warm to the touch. Stone is smoother and cooler in its effect, while smalti and glass are the most responsive to light.

mixed media

Combining two or more different materials is a way of adding drama, pattern and variety. Mixed media can achieve all kinds of exciting textural effects. Inserting pieces of broken china in an otherwise plain design adds not just colour and

far left A detail of a mosaiced garden seat, which provides durable external seating, by Celia Gregory. The stones make a break in the sections of the seating area.

left Iridescent, multi-faceted beads, shells and glass all contribute to the varied texture of this dramatic head by Takako Shimizu.

above The variations of the river-washed glass are very subtle in this mirror frame by Celia Gregory. The glass material has an uneven quality. Within the mosaic are trinkets of china, some of which come from pieces of pottery from the Tudor era.

left A close up of Norma Vondee's beautiful panel shows how the artist has depicted the sharp, spiky texture of a pineapple and included ridged glass along with rough and smooth ceramic pieces.

pattern: the broken pieces have a different texture and the fractured edges add spots of roughness to the even surface. You can contrast ceramic, which is slightly textured, with glass, which is smooth, or metal with stone. If you experiment with combinations of various textures, however, do not overload the mosaic with too many at the expense of clarity.

setting

Choose the texture according to the purpose of your mosaic. A splashback, kitchen countertop or cabinet door needs to throw off grease and water, not hold them. A floor or garden path should not be slippery underfoot, but nor should it be uneven so that people cannot walk on it without the risk of tripping. There is also an aesthetic aspect to choice of texture, so that it suits its setting. A rougher texture might look right in a farmhouse kitchen; but smoothness looks better in a more classical setting. The hardness of metallic is ideal in a contemporary loft-style interior. Stone and pebbles are a natural choice for a garden or garden room, but may not be what you want in a bedroom.

mosaic borders

To satisfy the eye, mosaics often need to be "finished off". Partly because they are three-dimensional, they generally require some sort of framing. Surrounding your design with a mosaic border is the ideal way to do this and many different styles have been developed over the years. You could even choose to make the edging the main focus of a mosaic by framing a plain central panel with a jazzy border.

The Greeks and Romans (and possibly other ancient cultures too) had pattern books of borders, often geometric, from which they could choose a desired design. Many of the most popular designs today can be traced back to those times, and some of them are shown on these pages. They are considered traditional, but successful, and work well with mosaic tesserae. The designs can be updated and executed in a more modern style.

choosing a border

When deciding upon which border to choose, adopt the same principles as when choosing a picture frame. The border should enhance the main image without distracting attention from it. It is generally advisable to keep the border simple, in colours related to the image but that are not too bright.

An alternative is to create a plain centre and concentrate all the drama in a bold border. The centre might be a regular design and essentially monochrome (for example, three or five shades of one soft colour), framed by a wide border of strong bold colours, different materials and a pronounced pattern. As ever, before committing yourself, sketch or draw up a fully coloured paper pattern beforehand and see whether you like the result.

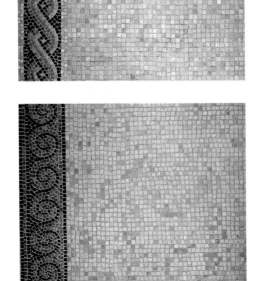
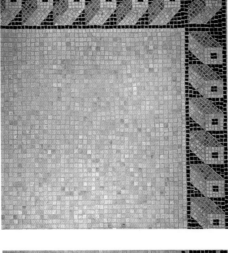

left, clockwise from top left **Stone mosaics** showing traditional border patterns in a guilloche or rope design, "Ishtar" pattern, a typical Greek key pattern and a Vitruvian-style scroll. Although ancient in design, these patterns are still frequently used and can be adapted to suit the needs of the modern mosaic artist.

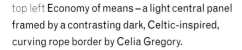

top left Economy of means – a light central panel framed by a contrasting dark, Celtic-inspired, curving rope border by Celia Gregory.

top right A wave-like mosaic pattern makes a decorative edge to these plain-coloured tiles.

above A brilliantly patterned border of a marble table by Salvatore Raeli.

right A rich, jewel-like border frames the mosaic and the colours are intensified by grouting the border in black. The border is built up with red vitreous glass tiles and in-between, patterns are created with mirror, glass jewels and different coloured tiles, by Celia Gregory.

walls and floors

buildings and mosaic

Many artists and architects around the world have employed mosaic on a grand scale to add decorative elements to façades of buildings. It can be used to make them more organic looking, or to soften harsh lines. It is frequently used to clad subways, or tower blocks and large exterior walls. Some architects have covered complete façades in mosaic, which then take on a sculptural quality.

Gaudí

Antoni Gaudí designed many houses and apartment blocks in Barcelona and the surrounding area, whose walls, balconies and roofs are a sinuous ocean of dips and curves decorated with mosaic tiles. His designs are practical and weather-resistant. Gaudí has used mosaic in such a way that it becomes not mere decoration but an intrinsic part of the structure that it adorns. Such a close blending of form and function, where the two become all but inseparable, is typical of the art movements that sprang up in the late 19th and early 20th centuries, an epoch when mosaic enjoyed one of its periodic revivals. Gaudí is still a major influence on contemporary mosaic artists.

Hundertwasser

The *Jugendstil* movement in Austria, which was concurrent with Art Nouveau, is one of the sources of inspiration for the contemporary Austrian artist and architect Friedensreich Hundertwasser (b.1928). More often known as a colourist painter, he draws inspiration from nature and uses art as decoration, creating rich surfaces with lots of vivid colour.

left Details of a mosaic-covered façade designed by Hundertwasser in Vienna, Austria.

In the mid-1980s in Vienna, he designed the eccentric museum *Hundert-wasserhaus* that houses a permanent exhibition of his paintings. The project involved integrating two old buildings. The bizarre façade is covered with mosaic and attracts coachloads of admiring tourists.

Among other features the house has undulating walls, Venetian balconies, onion domes, trees apparently sprouting from its walls, and irregularly shaped splashes of mosaic tiles. The building was devised along ecological principles and was intended as a blueprint for what was termed "humane living for the future".

La Défense

This notable development is a modern business area in Paris, France, where designers have lavished attention on surface decoration, including many mosaic-covered offices and fountains.

above The large, sculptural and organic-looking chimney stacks designed by Antoni Gaudí for the Casa Miló, often called *La Pedrera* (the quarry) in Barcelona, Spain.

left Bright mosaic tiles clad a group of office buildings and water features at La Défense, Paris, France.

exterior walls

Large and plain exterior walls present an irresistible opportunity for the decorator, and tough, weather-resistant mosaic is a clear choice. You may be tempted to ornament the exterior walls of the house, a dividing garden wall between you and your neighbour, or a low partition wall in a garden to separate flower or herb beds. All of nature can be your subject matter.

below left A wall fountain by Cleo Mussi made from recycled china.

below middle A stylized tree mosaic by Elaine M. Goodwin. Perfect when there is no room for the real thing.

below right A panel made from patterned china. Motifs are cut out and used as focal points for the patterns; some are raised to give extra emphasis.

On a practical note, do take into account that any mosaic that becomes an intrinsic part of the wall may have to stay when you move house. Remember, too, that while you may adore your mosaic of marine life, insects or whatever, it is very personal to you and will not be to the taste of every potential buyer.

maison Picassiette

These considerations did not in the least deter French gravedigger Raymond Isidore, however. Between 1930 and 1962 he mosaiced the outside of his modest home at 22 rue du Repos, Chartres, France

with bits of glass and broken crockery. This he fashioned into life-size images of himself, his wife and family, flowers, animals, birds and butterflies. Not content with adorning the outside in this way, Isidore beautified indoor walls, ceilings and even the furniture with designs fashioned from his foraging in scrapheaps.

walls

Isidore was not a man to let snags stand in his way, but for the less obsessed, the condition of walls can be an issue. Even more than indoors, outside walls often tend to be rough or uneven, particularly

old garden walls. A certain amount of unevenness is not a problem; in fact, the odd bump, kink or bulge can be the starting point of a design and can form a central part of it.

Truly dilapidated walls may be beyond the mosaicist's scope and may in fact be better left to be picturesquely ruined unless you are good at do-it-yourself or want to go to the expense of repairing or rebuilding them. But if they are smooth and in good condition, mosaic can add real flair in the garden or near the front door. Always choose materials that are weatherproof, such as stone, glass or frost-proof ceramic.

above The rose window, part of the garden in the extraordinary *Maison Picassiette*, the result of a lifetime's work for Raymond Isidore.

left A mosaic wall around the side of a garden pond. The broken china with the odd sea shell is set into a waterproof combined adhesive and grout, which was rubbed with a mixture of garden soil and pond water to blend the new with the old.

patio decoration

If you are not a great gardener, a mosaic can provide an evergreen, ever-colourful garden display that never needs looking after and will never fade with the seasons. For busy people, perhaps with a courtyard, a small town garden, a patio or a small roof terrace, a wall or panel of mosaic can create a stunning centrepiece. It can also divide a garden into different areas or spaces.

Gardens can be as much about creating effects as horticulture. To create an illusion of space, add a wall of reflective mosaic at the far end of the garden, or turn an ugly shed into an extra flowerbed by covering part or all of it with a pretty, soft mosaic design of foliage.

Gardeners often like to lead the eye to certain areas by adding structures to their gardens, such as seats, gazebos, pergolas or summerhouses. Unless you have the luxury (and the budget) of ordering an exclusive one-off commission, ready-made examples of these structures can still be turned into a truly individual feature. You can add mosaic inserts, panels or roundels to the surfaces of these small constructions.

Those lucky enough to have an old folly or grotto, especially if it is made from stone or concrete, can transform it into a place of enchantment by dotting the walls in its cool, dark depths with mirror mosaics, perhaps in the shape of stars or moons.

above left **A graphic mosaic sun and flowers brighten up this decorative garden wall.**

left **An outside dining area is defined by a mosaic frieze by Celia Gregory.**

opposite *La Via è incerta*: a tree poem by Elaine M. Goodwin, for a contemplative area of the garden.

interior walls

Walls in the home are perfect as settings for mosaic. It is possible to cover the entire area with mosaic or use it in the form of insets or panels. Mosaic can go almost anywhere but it is ideal in hardworking areas such as the hall, utility room, the conservatory or porch, the kitchen or bathroom.

below *The Sublime Wall*: created by Robert Grace from various sizes of mosaic sheets at the Gallery of Mosaic Art and Design.

Entire walls of mosaic can look beautiful and stunning. When planning such a feature, keep the elements of the design in scale with their setting: in the bathroom (right), the design as an entirety is composed of smaller patterns that can be absorbed by the eye at close quarters – there is no need to step back to try and see the whole. Different decorative schemes can be achieved with mosaic inside the home, from restful and intimate to bold and striking.

practicalities

If you want to apply mosaic directly to an interior wall, check first that the wall is strong enough to take the size and weight of mosaic and grout that you have in mind. Second, look carefully at the wall's surface. It need not necessarily be in perfect condition, but it must be even. Shine the strong raking light of a torch beam across the wall to show up areas of unevenness before you begin.

mirror

In some houses or apartments areas such as bathrooms can often be quite small and we know that using mirror is a good way to create the illusion of a space being much larger than it really is. However, where a whole mirrored wall might be a touch daunting, a fragmented wall of mirror mosaic is less revealing yet achieves the required illusion of space.

opposite **A stunning Moroccan-themed mosaic bathroom designed by Greg Williams, full of rich colour, rhythm and pattern.**

WALLS

walls

right A detail of a mirror ball and the musical notes that float in the wall of mosaic below.

below The musical notes emanating from the disc jockey in the centre of this mosaic by Celia Gregory appear to be exploding with sound.

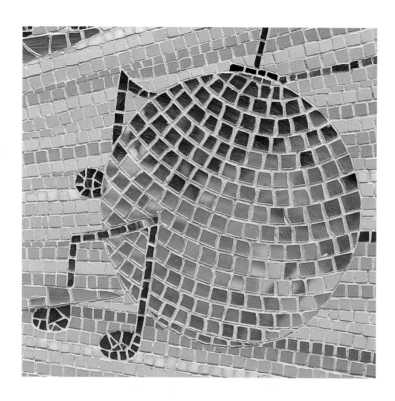

preparation

Surfaces need not necessarily be in perfect condition, but they must be even. Far from being covered up, having mosaic applied over the top will emphasize any unevenness, and the result will be disappointing and not pleasing to the eye.

In such cases, you have two choices. One is to prepare and even out the surface before applying the mosaic. The other is to make your mosaic as a separate panel or panels, that can be hung, like a picture, on the wall.

If walls are in a really bad state, you will need to steam off any paper, then remove the affected area of plaster. Mix new plaster and apply it to the affected

bathrooms

area according to the manufacturer's instructions, ensuring a good overlap with the sound part but making sure the new plaster is level with the old.

Allow to dry thoroughly (at least 24 hours in warm dry weather; longer in cooler or damper conditions), then smooth over with fine abrasive paper so that the new plaster and the join with the old are completely smooth.

bathrooms

Stone, marble and ceramic tile mosaics are a natural choice for bathrooms because of their resistance to damage or penetration by water and the choice is vast.

To make a bold statement, you could use mirror mosaic in the bathroom. It is glitteringly effective in this setting. Not only does it add a touch of Hollywood glitz that turns the daily shower into a special occasion and makes cleaning your teeth positively fun, it has wonderful light-reflecting qualities.

Most bathrooms are not over-endowed with natural daylight, and here mirror comes into its own. It is very well suited to artificial light, creating a feeling of space and brightness that will be enhanced when ripples of light are allowed to reflect off the moving surface of water on to the mosaic. This in turn will reflect the movement back in ever-shifting patterns on to other walls, the ceiling and perhaps the floor as well.

right The mosaic wall of small marble squares blends subtly with the Venetian basin carved from a solid piece of marble stone. It combines both traditional materials and elements of modern design.

decorative panels and friezes

More manageable in size than a complete mural, and a more realistic project for someone new to mosaic, decorative panels can go indoors or out. They can be incorporated into the structure or left separate, so that they can be removed and taken with you when you move. Also, when you redecorate, you may want to change the style of the room. Make the piece portable, if you have any doubts at all.

below left *Triangles*: an ungrouted mosaic in vitreous glass by Emma Biggs. Irregular and asymmetrical in design, the black and white triangles give the mosaic intensity.

below right Watery themes suit mosaic panel splashbacks in kitchens and bathrooms.

Since the great strength of mosaic is its impact, an entire wall covered in it may be more than you want. In such cases, the ideal solution is a decorative panel, specifically designed to suit its surroundings or its owner or both.

Mosaic insets and splashbacks can transform ordinary and standardized items such as kitchen units or countertops into something totally unique to you: be sure to make your design practical as it will receive much wear and tear. Mosaic also makes perfect splashbacks for cookers (stoves) and kitchen or bathroom sinks.

In such cases, an unfussy geometric design is ideal: in a kitchen, simple checks or plain colours with borders work well; in a bathroom you might like to suggest the movement of waves and water; in a bedroom, a trellis pattern in restful colours will suit. If you are aiming for something more personal, take the opportunity to devise an image that picks up on the room's colour scheme but incorporates elements

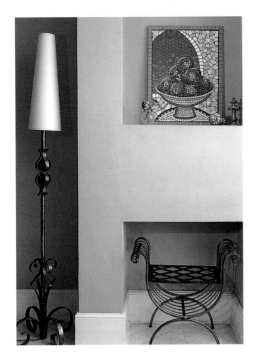

that are individual to you and your family, such as your initials, a favourite flower or a sporting symbol; in the case of growing children, choose some emblem or design that will not embarrass them in two or three years' time when their current craze has long faded!

Where walls are not in a good enough condition to allow a panel to be inset, a free-standing one makes a wonderful picture with depth and impact. Including a border into its design finishes off any mosaic, but if you want to heighten the impression of a work of art, consider having your mosaic panel framed before it is set in position.

bands and friezes

There are occasions when a minimal amount of decoration is all that is needed to transform an area of the house or garden. A frieze, or similar narrow band or border, may be more effective than a larger element in small spaces such as a downstairs cloakroom, a shower room, or in busy areas, such as a porch or hall-way, where too much elaboration tends to be overlooked amid the bustle of people

coming and going. You might want to replace the traditional dado (chair) rail with a simple but dramatic mosaic frieze. A border could echo the stair banister rail on the facing wall, or it could decorate a small galley kitchen or frame the front door or garden door – outside as well as in. A small mosaic could outline a window (perfect to highlight a porthole-style opening), a fire surround or mantelpiece.

A frieze or border can be equally effective at ground level. Such a simple device can form the perfect framing for a hearth or short flight of steps, again

above left A free-standing mosaic panel is all the decoration that is needed in an alcove. The colours echo the bronze of the furnishings, the walls and the lyre-shaped chair underneath.

above right *Gates of the Living*: maximum impact with minimum elaboration in this elegant panel by Elaine M. Goodwin.

indoors or out. Mosaic is also ideal for edging a garden path and is a good method of highlighting a pathway, giving a visual invitation to enter the garden and stroll around quietly enjoying its flowers, colours, scents and cool, green peace.

abstract colour panel

The spacing in this project is important; the tiles have been laid close together to allow the colours to relate to one another as directly as possible. Grout of a single colour can have a muting effect on a mosaic which is made with tiles across a range of tones, whereas an ungrouted mosaic like this one can look luminous and glowing. Grout is not always necessary on a wall panel inside the house.

materials and equipment

- **glass mosaic tiles in** various colours
- **wax crayons in** colours to match glass tiles
- **drawing paper**
- **tracing paper**
- **mosaic tile nippers**
- **MDF (medium-** density fiberboard) 50 x 50cm (20 x 20in)
- **black felt-tipped** pen
- **marker pens**
- **wood stain or dye** (colour optional) and brush
- **PVA (white)** adhesive
- **small brush for** applying glue

below The blocks between the grid are shades of grey, black, blue and white. Blocks overlaying these change shade. In turn, the shade and colour of the "ladders" alters depending on the block it overlaps.

1 Match the proposed tile colours to the crayons. This enables you to produce an accurate coloured drawing. As this scheme is fairly complex, a line drawing was produced as a plan for the coloured sketch.

2 Draw an accurate coloured sketch. To get a good idea of how the different blocks of tones and shading will work, put a layer of tracing paper over the line drawing and fill in the coloured areas. Cut the mosaic tiles in your chosen colours.

3 Draw the fundamentals of the design on to the board. It is not necessary to mark up any more detail than you see here. The segmented pattern is sketched in black felt-tipped pen, and the ladder lines in coloured permanent marker.

4 Paint or stain the frame of the board before starting to stick down the tiles.

5 Stick the tiles. Ensure you have a good quantity of PVA (white) glue applied to the board. Too thin and the tiles fail to adhere,

too much and the glue squeezes between the joints on to the tile face. Start by laying the coloured ladder shapes.

6 The principle behind this design is one of tonal colour changes, where boxes are laid within boxes. Sort your tiles into tones of greater or lesser intensity. Here, you can see one of the last blue/green boxes being laid. Using the direct method produces a slightly wobbly, light-reflective surface and although you notice the joints close-up, they do not detract from the finished effect of the piece.

mosaic pools

Mosaic is frequently used with water indoors and out, and baths, spas and pools are nearly always decorated with mosaic. Redolent of Hollywood in its heyday, the private pool is for many people a luxury, but the design possibilities are numerous if you are lucky enough to have the opportunity. Inspirational styles range from classical antiquity to traditional Turkish baths and opulent Edwardian and Victorian spas.

Whether private or public, most pool areas contain some element of mosaic decoration. This may be on columns or pillars, around the borders on the floors outside the pool, on nearby steps or paving, on tiles above the waterline, within the pool itself on the floor or sides, or in relaxation areas. Mosaic is waterproof and durable and these are obvious practical benefits, but there is a visual affinity between water and mosaic that is always pleasurable to see.

Roman baths are an obvious source of inspiration in pool design. Mythological subjects such as Neptune, sea serpents, water nymphs and mermaids are good mosaic motifs. Geometric borders and designs will also fit into such a classical scheme. High-ceiling pools that have been decorated with entirely handcrafted mosaic or marble almost compare with the awe-inspiring Byzantine cathedral ceilings in their overwhelming opulence and beauty.

Marine motifs such as dolphins and fish make popular and appropriate subjects for pools, likewise blues and greens are apt

left Sea-coloured mosaic panels link the pillars to the pool, easing the visual transition from stark white to blue.

left and below The mosaics add a wonderful quality to this lovely indoor swimming pool area by Celia Gregory. The cream walls and natural tones of the stone flooring allow the blue of the water to appear inviting and provide a good setting for the mosaic panel and urn. The simple border is inserted into luxurious marble stone flooring. It follows the edge of the pool, enhancing the shape and breaking up the tiles without competing with them.

colours and the tiles will impart a hue to the water. If there are designs on the floor of the pool or the sides, they should be sufficiently large enough to counterbalance the refraction and distortions of the water.

Old Victorian swimming pools and steam baths were decorated with beautiful painted ceramic tiles and some mosaic tiles. Modern pools are mainly lined with sheet mosaic of vitreous glass that is brilliant in colour and may have motifs of intricate mosaic. The growing range of mosaic tiles is constantly expanding the possibilities of pool design.

When applying mosaic tiles and sheets to pools, the base surface should be a mixture of sand and cement screed. The adhesive should be cement-based, frost-proof and water-proof. The direct and indirect methods are effective, but not working on to mesh. The tiles recommended are frost-proof glazed ceramic, vitreous glass and unglazed ceramic tiles when using the direct method, and frost-proof vitreous glass and unglazed ceramic tiles for the indirect method. Epoxy grout is suitable for underwater mosaics.

exterior flooring

Whether your garden is large, small or medium size, there is almost certain to be some kind of hard landscaping. Using mosaic for this is a good opportunity to create an individual, but practical flooring surface. Mosaic gives you the flexibility to use it as a display to rival the showiest of flowers, or to define different areas of the garden. Your designs can combine natural pebbles, pavers, tiles or stone materials.

below left This patio floor is mosaiced in different shades of smashed terracotta, and the walls of the flowerbeds are covered in smashed blue ceramic tiles.

below right Renaissance style at Dumbarton Oaks, Washington DC.

opposite A unusual water feature combined with stone mosaic.

Mosaic is becoming increasingly popular in gardens, where it can form part of the overall picture or be a major element in its own right. If you are planning to use mosaic at ground level out of doors, take advice on drainage and how to ensure surfaces are able to throw off rainwater and yet be level for walking on. There should be a "fall" or the surface should be slightly tilted so water will run off.

Mosaic works well in the natural light of the exterior environment, blends in with plants, is long lasting and, because of its waterproof nature, it can be used extensively in the garden.

hard landscaping

Mosaic floors and paths work well in low-maintenance gardens as they provide decorative hard landscaping. Mosaic can be applied to other garden features to co-ordinate with the floor, such as pots, retaining walls, in-built sculptural seats or water features.

Stone and pebble mosaics are excellent choices for covering large floor areas. Broken ceramic tiles enliven smaller areas. Add mosaic squares to patios to introduce colour and interest. In larger, formal gardens, you may want to lay a classical mosaic piazza or courtyard area.

snakes and ladders floor

This is an interactive mosaic game for children of all ages and adults too. It was designed and made, with help from Norma Vondee, by a large group of children aged 11 to 16. The ancient tradition of games, paths and puzzles in mosaic gives this simple, strong design an ageless appeal. The background is quick and easy to do, so you can really express yourself with vibrant colour in the swirling design of the snakes. You can lay a border of blue tiles around the finished floor if you wish and you can also size the design to fit into your garden or outdoor space, or cover a patio, as here.

materials and equipment

- paper
- felt-tipped pens
- tape measure
- scissors
- thick marker pen
- clear plastic film
- fibreglass mesh
- mosaic tile nippers
- vitreous glass
  mosaic tiles
- waterproof PVA
  (white) glue
- rubber gloves
- patio cleaner
- black stain
- cement-based
  adhesive
- notched trowel
- sand
- cement

1 Draw up a masterplan for the whole board. Play a game on it to make sure that it works.

2 Measure out one of the outside paving slabs to be covered. Cut out 25 pieces of paper to fit. Fold them into quarters and mark out the sections. These are your 100 squares for the game.

3 Copy out your design on to the paper using a thick marker pen.

4 Cover the front of each square with clear plastic and then a piece of mesh, cut to size.

5 Outline each of the 100 squares with matt black tiles, cut in half. Use waterproof PVA (white) glue to stick them to the mesh. Outline the numbers with quarter tiles and the snakes with half and quarter tiles.

6 Fill in the snakes and ladders with glossy, brightly coloured tiles of your choice.

7 Fill in the background squares with varying colours – even numbers in shades of white, odd numbers in shades of blue. Leave the squares to dry overnight, then turn them over, peel off the paper and the plastic film used to protect the paper and leave until totally dry. Make sure all the tiles are stuck on to the fibreglass mesh and readhere any that fall off.

8 Wearing gloves, clean all the paving slabs with patio cleaner and rinse well. Add a black stain to a cement-based adhesive, following the manufacturer's instructions, and apply a thin, even layer to each square with a notched trowel.

right Direct methods of laying mosaic involve placing the material straight on to the working surfaces. This snakes and ladders mosaic is made using the indirect method. The indirect techniques involve working on to mesh or paper off-site and fitting the mosaic later. The tiles are laid on to mesh, which is then laid on to the patio and grouted. You can cement the mosaic on to different types of surfaces, such as paving stones, but make sure it is flat and even.

snakes and ladders

right Children and adults alike can play on this fun mosaic patio floor. Players throw dice to move around the board; if you land on a ladder you move up to the connecting square and if you land on a snake, you slip back down.

9 Lay on the design, one section at a time, allowing for gaps between the slabs. Mark all the pieces clearly and refer to the plan often as you work. Tamp down the squares gently and evenly. Leave to dry completely.

10 Grout the mosaic, using a mixture of sand and cement with an added black stain. Wipe off excess and allow to dry out slowly.

paths and paving

These are designed to lead people from one part of the garden to another and provide an area on which to walk, stand or sit. Mosaic can add decorative touches and draw the eye toward a certain spot in the garden or vista. Stone, hard tiles, such as terracotta, crazy paving and pebbles are among the best choices for garden pathways and paving, as they are hardwearing.

below left **A** Celtic design in contrasting stone between two areas of path.

below middle **A** simple repetition of three shapes in the same colours creates a three-dimensional effect in this path.

below right **A** diamond-shaped mosaic suits this formal garden.

Paths may conveniently serve to divide one area from another, but in heavily planted gardens they should not intrude visually into the overall design, or it will become over-busy and disjointed. Here, the subdued natural colours of stone and pebbles are ideal.

pebble mosaics

As we have seen, pebbles were the basis of the very earliest mosaics, used as flooring thousands of years ago. At the time, it was easy and practical to use a material that was plentiful and durable in the extreme. Pebble mosaics have a lovely textured surface, they are comfortable to walk on and gradually, with age, they acquire an attractive polished sheen.

There are certain things to consider when laying pebble mosaics. You will need a firm base to bed them in and there must be a support all around them. Pebbles should be placed vertically so that a small surface is open to the air and they should be tightly packed, so there is virtually no movement between individual stones.

You also need to be careful when choosing pebbles. Certain types are more durable than others, such as cylindrical, longish limestone and granite pebbles (sometimes known as "longs" or "skimmers"), sandstone flat-tops, granite cylinders and some flint, quartz or black basalt pebbles.

stone mosaics

Gravel and stone vary in colour from one area of a country to another. Though it is perfectly possible to buy stone in whatever colour you choose from suppliers, selecting stone or pebbles that come from the area in which you live will produce natural and pleasing results, which will also blend successfully with any brick house walls or old garden walls of brick or stone. When choosing stone, durability is paramount: the stone must not be porous or inclined to break. Colour and shape are also important considerations: some variation is pleasing but it is best to make sure contrasts are not extreme or the overall effect will be diluted.

Remember to see what stone or pebbles look like wet as well as dry. Dark stone, for example, can look contemporary and sophisticated when dry; when wet, it turns even darker in colour and may be too gloomy if your garden receives little sun or is obscured by tall trees.

Outdoor mosaic work with pebble or stone takes a significant investment in time and effort. Stone is heavy, and it will be hard work, with lifting, bending and kneeling. It is a sensible precaution to practise beforehand on a small area such as a step, patio inset, or even a path or bed

edging. If necessary, get a professional mosaic artist to design and undertake larger projects, as they can probably work much faster than you can.

In addition, remember the environmental issues when obtaining your stones and pebbles. Many shingle beaches are

above This bright mosaic of blue glazed tile fragments highlights the maritime theme along with sea-washed stones and spiky planting.

suffering serious erosion from people helping themselves: make sure you go to a reputable supplier.

interior flooring

Floors, whether they are indoors or out, take a pounding. But mosaic, as we have seen, is durable and long lasting: several examples now around 2,000 years old are still in very good condition. Hallways, garden rooms, kitchens, utility rooms and bathrooms are obvious choices for mosaic, but it can also furnish living rooms without seeming too cold or hard to walk on.

Mosaic is a practical flooring choice for most areas, being versatile and hard-wearing. Most mosaic materials are tough; they resist marks, spills, scuffs and stains and, just as important, they are not inclined to fade over time. With the right preparation, they will adhere to most surfaces and be comfortable underfoot.

right Mosaic flooring is practical and hard-wearing in a hall and the Greek key border suits this imposing Victorian style.

opposite The colours are allowed to speak for themselves in this unfussy, but boldly decorated bathroom.

working on whole floors

Any floor finish must be able to withstand feet, shoes, paws, claws and perhaps wheels as well. A mosaic may be all the decoration a floor needs: ornamentation does not always need to be at eye level to be effective, and treating your room scheme in this way can make a striking and refreshing change. There is no reason at all why you should not mosaic a whole floor, but be aware that it is a major undertaking, requiring many hours of patient and skilled work. Alternatively, an inset is an effective way of achieving almost the same result with a fraction of the work.

Choose good hardwearing materials that are proof against the risk of damage. Stone and suitably glazed clay are ideal; glass is less so for obvious reasons, although it can be used with care. The floor must be level and even when you lay the mosaic surface and be level for walking.

It is important to remember scale when designing for floors. The eye will not want so much detail at this distance, either in the design itself or in the size of stone or tesserae: ensure they are not too small or the overall result will appear too fussy. Large sections of colour with bold elements such as central motifs and borders will work well.

creative effects

Mosaic can be used on a large scale in a domestic setting. In the bathroom, whole floors and walls can be covered, or you can be less dramatic and cover just the floor. You could also cover the skirting (base) board and link the floor to the walls. The colour palette available is vast, especially if using vitreous glass mosaic sheets. You could choose to echo interior details, such as stained glass in a window, or to co-ordinate the mosaic with other features in the room, such as the colour of the curtains or the bathroom suite.

For hallways, you may choose to work within a more muted colour palette, such as a soft green to balance a rich terracotta mosaic floor. On a porch, a warm shade also creates a welcoming feel. Try dividing a large floor area into sub-sections with the use of decorative borders, which help to lead the eye through from the door along the corridors to the foot of the stairs.

above Classic black and white tiles are enlivened by a floor inset of mosaic in a stylized reptile and ivy leaf design by Elaine M. Goodwin.

far left Diamonds of stone and rough-textured pebbles would be perfect in a cottage or farmhouse.

left In total contrast to pebble, this mosaic floor is as smooth as a carpet.

floors

left **A cool and restful ambience is conjured up by using coffee-coloured mosaic flooring with white grouting, which complements the white sanitary ware.**

below **Sea-inspired designs, such as sailing boats, shells or fish, are naturally at home in the bathroom.**

Mosaic has a natural affinity with and suitability for bathrooms. Try using it in different ways. Soft, creamy colours and an elegant border will create a restful decorative scheme and a room to relax in. Marine life and nautical themes fit well into a bathroom scheme.

Think about what mosaic can do in living areas, too. A small mosaic, such as a hearth, can be laid to give a sophisticated, smooth surface and create a focal point in a room. Black and white is a classic colour combination for tiled kitchen floors and can be livened up with a smart mosaic inset. If you have a quarry tile floor, a warm, terracotta mosaic would suit.

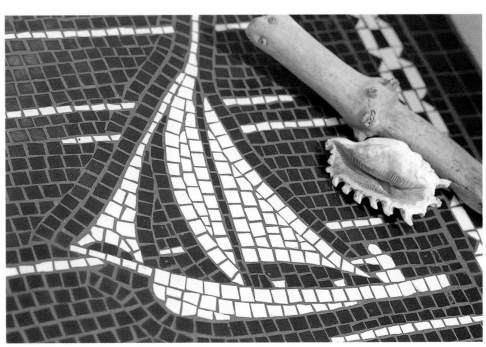

mosaic hearth

This hearth has been decorated using the reverse indirect technique in which tiles are laid face down on brown paper. This is used when it is essential to have a smooth mosaic. Using this technique, the work can be done off-site, which is beneficial if the mosaic is situated in a location where it is inconvenient to work on to it directly. The reverse method is good for ensuring a flat finish when working with uneven tiles, but not practical when working with tiles that only have the coloured glaze on one side, as the tile is laid in reverse and would therefore not be visible.

materials and equipment

- chisel and hammer
- brown paper
- craft (utility) knife
- scissors
- sweeping brush
- sponge
- PVA (white) glue
- water
- piece of wooden board
- adhesive tape
- pencil and ruler
- coloured vitreous glass tiles
- mosaic tile nippers
- matt cream porcelain tiles
- small brush
- grey powdered adhesive
- mixing bowls and buckets
- notched trowel
- wire (steel) wool
- screwdriver
- rubber gloves
- grout

1 Using a chisel and hammer, remove any old tiles from the fireplace.

2 Chisel away any remaining tile cement. It is essential to have a very smooth surface on which to lay the mosaic.

3 To make a template, take a piece of brown paper, larger than the area to be mosaiced, and fold over the edges to fit exactly. It can be tricky around the more detailed areas.

4 Using a craft (utility) knife and scissors, cut out the shape accurately. Check it by placing it back into the hearth.

5 Brush away any loose debris from the fireplace. Seal the concrete by sponging on a mix of one part PVA (white) glue to five parts water. Allow to dry.

6 This technique works in reverse, so turn the template upside down. Place the template on a piece of wooden board and stick it down with adhesive tape to ensure that the paper does not move around.

7 Draw out border edging. Mark straight lines with a pencil and ruler; the first line at 1mm ($\frac{1}{16}$in) in from the edge of the paper (this allows a margin of error when fitting),

and the second at 2.1cm (¾in) in from the edge of the paper, another at 7.1cm (2¾in) and again at 9.1cm (3½in). You should now have 5cm (2in) for the detail between the two dark purple bands. Take care that the lines meet neatly at corners. Stick strips of dark purple border tiles with PVA glue along the two narrow bands, paper-side down. The bulk of the design is made up of sheets of vitreous glass; cut them up with a craft knife and put them in position. Fill as much of the space as possible with whole tiles, paper-side down. Here, paler shades

of the purple are used. If there are gaps, probably at the back and sides of the mosaic, clip tiles to fit and stick them later.

8 The detail of the border is made from matt cream porcelain tiles clipped into quarters. Position these in a central line that runs parallel to the two strips of dark purple vitreous glass. Take care that the lines meet neatly at their corners. Then, starting in one corner, make a grid with cut quarters of cream tile at 2.5cm (1in) intervals inside the two dark purple bands. Fill in the gaps with a

variety of colours from the vitreous glass range, clipped into quarters. To ensure the correct spacing, lay the tiles down before you stick them in position. Adjust the spacing so that the uniformed design works, taking particular care in the corners.

9 Using a small brush, apply PVA glue to the front of the small tiles, and stick them on to the paper.

▷

mosaic hearth

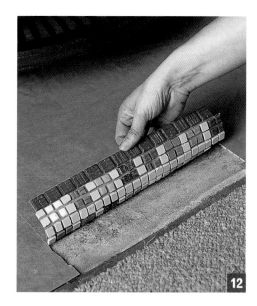

10 Apply PVA glue to the paper on the back of the sheets of light purple tiles and stick them on to the brown paper. Leave the completed mosaic to dry for several hours.

11 Cut up the mosaic into manageable pieces and lift them up, shake gently to remove tile fragments and any loose tiles. Stick these back in place with PVA glue.

12 Back on-site, lay the sections of the mosaic, tile-side down. It should fit, and all you will see is brown paper.

13 Lay the sheets to one side, so the order in which they need to be laid is obvious. Mix up some grey powdered adhesive with water at a ratio of one part adhesive to four parts water. Apply the adhesive to the concrete surface with a notched trowel; ensure you have a good even bed. Carefully lay down the sheets, tile-side down. Once you are happy with the positioning of the sheets, press them into the adhesive and rub over the surface with a damp sponge. Leave to dry for 24 hours.

14 Fill a bucket with warm water and, using a sponge, dampen the brown paper. Leave for 5 minutes, then dampen again.

15 When the paper is ready to be removed it should peel off easily. Some bits will stick but these can be cleaned off with wire (steel) wool. Wash down the mosaic and glue back any pieces that may have come loose.

16 There is a tendency with this technique for adhesive to squeeze up between the gaps and it tends to be a different colour from the grout. Clear this excess away with a screwdriver or pointed tool.

17 Wearing gloves, mix up a grey grout following the manufacturer's instructions and grout the mosaic. Allow it to dry and remove excess grout with a damp sponge. The mosaic has a simple, contemporary feel with a strong use of colour, bringing a new lease of life to this old fireplace.

furniture and ornament

mosaic tables

The humble table top is an ideal surface for any mosaicist, especially beginners, being flat and at a convenient height to be seen and admired. As a decorative technique, mosaic is well suited to tables and is relatively easy to do, given that a good, even horizontal surface is presented ready to work on. You can also experiment with applying tiles using both the direct and indirect methods.

above left The strong rope design mosaic by Celia Gregory suits the square robustness of this coffee table.

above right Beautiful strips of abstract stained glass mosaic in vibrant colours make this an imposing dining table, by Christopher Skinner and Max Reeve.

Relatively inexpensive complete tables are available from junk shops and a mosaic is an imaginative and fulfilling way of transforming these pieces into something personal. A chess or games table, side, hall, occasional, telephone or bedside table, perhaps even a dressing table would be perfect for mosaic.

You can easily make your own table tops from MDF (medium-density fiberboard), plyboard or other manufactured boards, and you can create different shapes and sizes to suit your mosaic design by cutting it out with a jigsaw or a circular saw. Sand down any rough fibres.

The edge of the table can be finished in mosaic or have a stainless steel rim or similar edging. Sand down any sharp mosaic edges to avoid catching clothes. You can buy simple metal bases or frames to support the table tops from second hand (thrift) stores, get a blacksmith to make one, commission a craftsperson to make a one-off piece, or even make your own from blocks of wood.

table surfaces

You need to make sure that the finished result is smooth and even. You could mosaic the entire table top or you may prefer to insert a decorative panel into a part of it, often the centre. A mosaic border around the edge would look very attractive. Such panels or borders must be

flush or level with (not above or below) the rest of the table top and this should be taken into account at the design stage.

To ensure that the surface remains even, if you want to insert a mosaic panel, you will need to calculate what depth the finished work will be, remove that amount from the depth of the table top and sink the mosaic into the prepared area.

Make sure that the final result is smooth and even: people must be able to put things down, such as drinks, without them toppling over or wobbling precariously. Non-porous materials, such as glazed clay, glass or a suitable stone can be easily wiped dry without becoming stained. If the material you choose is porous, you could cover the entire surface of your design with a protective layer of glass. Ask a specialist to cut this to size.

Your choice of design is personal, but repeated patterns and continuous swirling or abstract designs work particularly well on circular tables. You could try a Celtic knot motif or an Islamic organic design. There are many pattern books available in craft shops to look for inspiration. The late Victorians were great pattern book makers and in these, you will find an abundance of choice for border designs.

above left This table top by Elizabeth De'Ath is decorated with mosaic mirror, divided into sections and bands to create a distinct pattern.

above right An Islamic-influenced table top and a roundel mosaic in similar patterns by Elaine M.Goodwin.

right Celtic designs have a timeless quality that suits both modern and traditional furniture.

stained glass table

The designs of Hundertwasser inspired this table. His mosaics were laid in shapes inset on a surface, rather than over the entire area, and he was equally aware of the spaces that lay between the mosaic. In this project too, the veneer forms are as important as the mosaic. The lines give the table a sensual and dynamic feeling, while the stainless steel edging creates a contemporary finish.

materials and equipment

- **110 x 70cm (43 x 28in) MDF (medium-density fiberboard),** 18mm (⅜in) thick
- soft pencil and eraser
- tracing paper
- scissors
- iron
- oak wood veneer, 3mm (⅛in) thick
- craft (utility) knife
- table top and legs
- stained glass tiles, 3mm (⅛in) thick: red, iridescent pink and rippled clear glass (colours optional)
- scrap paper
- chestnut wood dye (stain)
- paintbrush
- rubber gloves
- clear polyurethane varnish
- **PVA (white) glue**
- small brush
- bowl
- contact adhesive
- clamps
- grout
- red grout dye (stain)
- sponge
- glass cleaner
- **18mm (¾in)** stainless steel edging

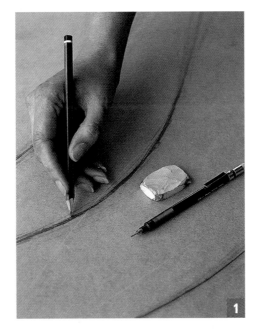

1 On the piece of MDF (medium-density fiberboard), draw wavy lines with a soft pencil down the length of the board. These make three bands that will be filled with stained glass and four bands of the veneer.

2 Trace the lines on to tracing paper. Then cut out four templates for the veneer. The veneer should be 3mm (⅛in) thick, the same as the stained glass.

3 Iron the cut-out templates flat, using a warm heat, as the tracing paper tends to crinkle and fold.

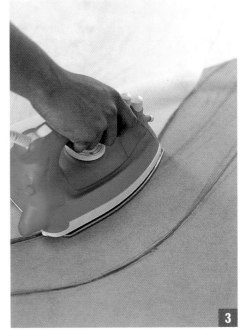

left The soft, wavy lines of this table work well in a minimalist living space, complementing the angles of the room, the concrete floor and the design of the accessories.

stained glass table

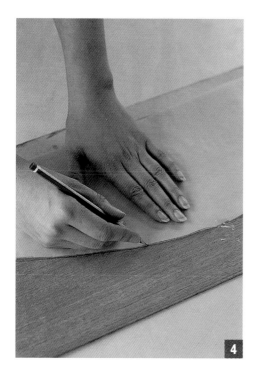

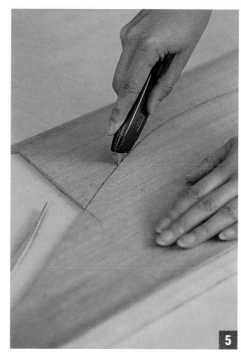

4 Place the templates on to the oak veneer. Using a soft pencil, carefully draw a line around the edge of each piece of tracing paper. It makes it easier for cutting to place any straight lines along the straight edge of the veneer.

5 With the sharp blade of a craft (utility) knife, score a strong line along the pencil marks. Work the curved line in sections, removing excess veneer as you go.

6 Place the four cut-out sections of veneer in their correct positions on the table. Make a selection of colours in the stained glass tiles; use warm tones such as red, pink and clear rippled glass that will pick up the tone of the beige wood and contrast beautifully with the dense quality of veneer.

7 Lay the pieces of veneer on to paper and stain with a red chestnut wood stain or a tone that has a red tint and a darker colour. Wearing gloves, apply two thin coats and allow to dry. Apply several coats of varnish, allowing each coat to dry before applying the next; follow the manufacturer's instructions.

8 Place the veneer panels back in position on the table. Cover the back of the stained glass evenly with PVA (white) glue, using a small brush. Lay the pieces in a random arrangement on the table in a ratio of four red tiles to every two pink and one clear. PVA glue is white but it dries clear.

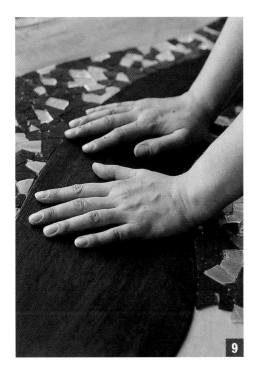

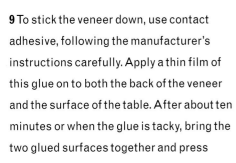

above Waves of glass give vibrancy to the design.

9 To stick the veneer down, use contact adhesive, following the manufacturer's instructions carefully. Apply a thin film of this glue on to both the back of the veneer and the surface of the table. After about ten minutes or when the glue is tacky, bring the two glued surfaces together and press down hard, clamp and leave to dry. Once the two glued surfaces have made contact, no repositioning is possible – so take care!

10 Wearing gloves, carefully grout the mosaics with a grey powder grout mixed with red dye. Clean off the excess and take care not to get any grout on the veneer. When it is nearly dry, go over it with a sponge dipped in glass cleaner to remove excess grout. When completely dry, glue the stainless steel edging in position around the table.

decorative accessories

Home accessories offer a limitless supply of design opportunities for the mosaicist. In the bedroom, you might choose to ornament a jewellery box, a storage or linen chest, a wall or dressing table mirror or even a curtain pelmet. Or in the lounge, you could display mosaic photo frames, a fire screen, a letter rack, a clock or a decorative table lamp. In the kitchen, mosaic herb pots would make a very pretty addition to the room.

below left **Gentle** spiralling bands of mosaic cover this tall terracotta urn. Small chips of gold smalti give the piece extra highlights.

below right **Fresh** pots of herbs in the kitchen become decorative objects in their own right, and good enough to display on the table.

Mosaic is an effective disguise, transforming the mundane or mass-produced into something original. Containers make excellent subjects for mosaic decoration. Plant pots, terracotta urns, candle holders, vases and bowls are just a few suggestions.

smaller accessories

These do not require a huge commitment in terms of time or effort or cost of materials. They are good items on which to practise your ideas and techniques and

each project can be closely monitored. Objects can be functional or purely decorative.

An inexpensive, plain wooden photograph frame, a pot stand or a house number plaque would be ideal choices to start with since they are regular in shape, can be laid flat and are easy to work with. A set of table mats or coasters with varying designs would be an easy way of experimenting with colour and patterns before embarking on larger projects.

Excellent hunting grounds for objects to mosaic – such as picture frames, plain wooden boxes, old cans and pots, and larger pieces such as simple chairs and tables – are car boot sales, junk (curio) shops and even house clearance auctions. "Job lot" boxes of assorted odds and ends can be picked up extremely cheaply.

Make a contemporary mosaic bowl by buying a shallow, light, wooden, metal or plastic shape to which you can adhere mosaic to on the inside only. This will give you a stable base.

Frames can be made from many diverse materials that can be customized with mosaic; they can be flat or include three-dimensional or sculptural elements. They provide an excellent platform for self-expression and you can explore combinations of colour and texture and create collage-like effects.

moving components

When tackling a piece of furniture that has movable parts, such as drawers or doors, you need to make sure that the tesserae do not impede the movement of the components once they are applied and grouted. Always check the space available and align the tesserae evenly, so that they do not overlap. Scrape away surface cement on inside edges with a sharp, flat instrument. Make sure all excess grout is wiped away.

If you are designing a clock, you must first find a way of accommodating the mechanism that works the hands. Then you should design the surface decoration to allow for the function of the clock and movement of the hands.

above A large, striped, stained glass mosaic bowl by Martin Cohen.

left Squares of textured, coloured glass cast beautiful patterns when a candle is lit in this mosaic candle holder.

chests and cabinets

Most of us have a chest in the hall or in a guest room into which all sorts of odds and ends are pushed. Store-bought pieces can benefit from the application of a little decoration: in the case of chests, matching panels on the lid and front; or on chests of drawers (bureaux), small matching or related motifs on each drawer will turn the ordinary into the unusual. Make sure that the joints and hinges of the furniture and the floor can withstand the weight of the mosaic as it can be very heavy.

dressers and units

Think about adding mosaic to the doors of kitchen units, a bathroom cabinet or a dresser. You do not have to cover the whole

furniture

left Four women are linked and dance around this very large urn by Celia Gregory. The pot is designed to look aged, cracked and fragmented like an antique.

below left The daisy-filled panels of this pine bedhead would look beautiful in a country-style bedroom. Use the same design to decorate other panelled furniture.

door; a small panel would suffice. Mosaic is an inventive way of reviving and personalizing otherwise mass-produced items or finds in secondhand stores.

home office

Desks, computer tables, filing cabinets and other home office furniture could benefit from mosaic panels or inserts. Remember that such pieces must do the job for which they are intended: computer tables should form a wobble-free base for the equipment; filing cabinets must have drawers that open and close; and it has to be possible to write and read easily at a desk. Adding personal touches in the form of mosaics – perhaps incorporating some symbol, logo or initials connected to the business – is a good way of making functional areas less intrusive in the rest of the living space.

screens

A screen is the perfect solution to divide a room into different areas. As useful as they are, screens need a touch of lightness to stop them becoming too slab-like; apart from Japanese-style examples of parchment and pale wood frame, the average screen can look like a solid wall. Consider using mirror or, if you do not want reflections, gold, silver or other metallic materials in geometric and abstract designs. The play of light, natural or artificial, will add mystery, lightness and movement.

Fire screens are also easy to make. You could buy a ready-made one from a good craft shop or cut a screen shape from plywood using a jigsaw, and then slot it into custom-made feet.

storage racks

Storing coats or keys can be a problem, but you can make the rack an interesting feature by adding mosaic. The base can be made from MDF (medium-density fiber-board) or plywood, which can be cut into any size or shape you like. Add the support fixtures, such as hooks or mirror plates, with which to hang the rack before adding the mosaic. Mark out the positions for the coat or key hooks and screw them on after you have grouted and cleaned the mosaic.

above A golden stained-glass mosaic fire screen: the stained glass was laid on top of clear glass so that light can still shine through. Bands of colour flow freely in waves across the panels, giving a real sense of movement.

left *Tutti I Frutti:* a picture frame and mirror with abstract geometric patterns of brightly coloured stained glass, by Anna Tabata Cominitti.

mirror frames

One of the most popular subjects for mosaic is the mirror frame; the variety of effects shown here gives an indication why. Mirrors are useful objects for practical reasons, but also for decorative ones. Any room, however small, benefits from the addition of a mirror, as an attractive accessory in its own right, to increase the sense of space and to reflect light back into the room. In addition, there is an affinity between the textural and reflective qualities of mirror and mosaic, so they combine together well.

right A large, curved mirror inspired by the painting of Gustav Klimt, which is reflected in the shape of the design, and the use of flowing lines of gold smalti broken up in a rhythmic pattern, which makes a very decorative and individual piece by Norma Vondee.

Frames can be as extravagantly or simply shaped as you want. You can buy ply boards or MDF (medium-density fiber-board) boards in circular or square shapes and mosaic them to your required designs. Or you may well want to design your own shape, perhaps even with a raised or curved outline, which can be cut with a circular saw or jigsaw.

opposite This large, curvaceous mirror by Celia Gregory was made from washed glass collected from the banks of the River Thames, and contrasts with the angular shape of the fireplace. The soft greens beautifully complement the whites and neutral tones of the room.

left A pair of complementary circular mirrors, given extra interest by placing the mirror off-centre.

right A floral mosaic mirror and table top. The design and colours of the mirror and accompanying table top could match, or, as here, echo each other without repeating exactly.

mirror mosaic

This geometric mosaic uses contrasting colours of glass and ceramic tiles to create a stunning wall panel. Mirror and gold tiles add an opulent, reflective feel. Hang this mosaic in a bathroom where the mirror tiles will reflect the bath water, or in a hallway to make a dramatic focal point.

materials and equipment

- pencil
- ruler
- piece of **MDF** (medium-density fiberboard), 9mm (⅜in) thick, cut to 46 x 46cm (18 x 18in)
- large paintbrush
- **PVA (white) glue**
- mirror adhesive
- mirror, cut to 19.5 x 19.5cm (7¾ x 7¾in)
- **vitreous glass and matt ceramic mosaic tiles**
- mosaic tile nippers
- small paintbrush
- mirror tiles
- grout
- grout container
- grout spreader
- sponge or cloth

1 Using a pencil and ruler, divide the board so that there are seven equal spaces along each edge. Join up your marks carefully to form a grid. Mark the alternate squares with a pencil squiggle to show where the different squares of tones will be mosaiced.

2 Using a large paintbrush, seal the board with a coat of PVA (white) glue diluted 50/50 with water. Allow to dry thoroughly.

3 Using mirror adhesive, stick the main mirror on to the centre of the board so that there are even borders all around it. Leave it to dry.

4 Cut the gold vitreous glass and the two shades of ceramic mosaic tiles in half with the mosaic tile nippers. Squeeze the nippers firmly for a clean cut.

5 Starting on the squares marked with the pencil squiggles, stick the tiles in position, alternating between a light shade of vitreous glass and a light shade of matt ceramic. Leave a slight gap between each piece. Paint undiluted PVA glue on to each square and stick the tiles to fit within the pencil guidelines.

6 Finish sticking these lighter squares over the entire board, working carefully to ensure the gaps between each piece remain even.

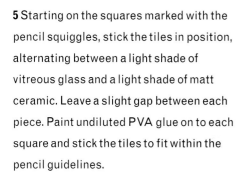

7 Cover the alternate squares over the entire board with two darker colours, sticking them in position as before.

8 Stick the mirror tiles in the centre of the darker squares using mirror adhesive.

▷

right Two differently toned
variations of the same
style mirror echoing the
soft, warm tones of
the wooden floor and
soft furnishings.

mirror mosaic

9 Stick the gold tiles in the centre of the lighter squares using PVA glue. Allow to dry.

10 Mix the grout to a creamy consistency, following the manufacturer's instructions, and spread it out evenly over the board, making sure the gaps between the tiles have been filled. Smooth a little grout around the edge of the board. With a slightly damp sponge or cloth, wipe away any excess grout from the surface and from the edge of the board. Leave to dry.

garden furniture

Mosaic works extremely well on furniture and features in the garden. A window box, chair or bench is perhaps not the first item that you might think of applying mosaic to, but it makes a real focal point. Adding mosaic is a wonderful way to revive tired or battered pieces of furniture and you will also make pieces more weather-resistant. Permanent structures can be built and covered in mosaic, such as a bird bath.

seating

Choose a style of seat, chair or bench that is suitable for mosaic decoration. Cheap and cheerful white plastic garden furniture cannot be made into works of art, but a simple kitchen-style chair is an ideal candidate for treatment. As far as benches go, it is best to leave old and pretty wrought iron, metal or teak wooden benches in their original condition. However, just as with tables and chairs, a standardized garden bench can be decorated to great effect.

Almost any part of a chair or bench can take mosaic. You may wish to mosaic the seat or the arms (if the piece has them); equally the back is an ideal setting. If it is for sitting on or against, ensure that the mosaic is flush, smooth and even; you do not want sharp edges digging into tender parts of the anatomy, tearing threads in clothing or catching the spine at the wrong point.

preparation

Think carefully about the amount of mosaic materials required: covering an entire chair, or a set of chairs, will take a large amount of tesserae, and in both cases the element of unity is important.

There should be continuity of pattern or colour to avoid the end result looking disjointed. Pieces do not need to be identical, but they must have some strong

left An old chair is given a new lease of life by adding mosaic. A large, three-dimensional object will require a deceptively large amount of tesserae to cover it. If you do not have a lot of raw material in the same pattern, use slightly different patterns in the same colour to overcome this.

left Funky mosaic "cushions" of abstract faces for a garden bench by Cleo Mussi; a great fun idea to create a focal point in a plain courtyard or contemporary setting.

below An unobtrusive mosaic birdbath by Sheryl Wilson blends into the surrounding foliage.

bottom The sculptured seat covered in blue mosaic brings life and colour to this city patio.

visual factor linking them, and this is most successfully done with colour or pattern. If you are in doubt, it is best to start with just one item, or one section of an item. Lay your chosen pieces out on a dry, flat surface, in the design you have planned, to make sure you are happy with size, position, shade and shape before mixing up the setting medium.

There are no restrictions on what you can mosaic in the garden. You could even build a small fantastical grotto, covered with shells and small pebbles, mirror or semi-precious stones.

uni garden seat

Uni or sea urchins are found clinging to wild, rocky shorelines or nestling in rock pools. Their simple, pleasing shapes bring a taste of the ocean to your garden or patio. They are found in nature in a rainbow of colours, such as soft green, pink, coral, orange, maroon, purple and the soft blue or lavender illustrated here. This shape could be adapted to become a low, wide seat, used as a piece of sculpture in a garden, or even drilled and plumbed to become a fountain.

materials and equipment

- 4 whole breezeblocks (cinderblocks) and 1 small cut piece
- sand
- cement
- protective goggles and gloves
- hammer
- cold chisel
- charcoal
- vitreous glass or stoneware tiles
- cement-based adhesive
- black stain
- notched trowel
- mosaic tile nippers
- slate
- glass baubles, silver and glass circles or stones

above **Plan the colours and materials of your design before starting work on your mosaic.**

1 Mortise together four lightweight breeze-blocks (cinderblocks) with sand and cement. Put a cut block in the centre. Leave to dry.

2 Wearing protective goggles and gloves, knock off the corners of the blocks with a hammer and cold chisel. Continue to shape the blocks into a flat dome.

3 Using charcoal, draw a line on to each side to give the impression of a rounded sea urchin. Draw lines radiating out from the centre. Keep your choice of colours simple and bold. Lay out the design before you start and apply the tiles to check the spacing. The tiles must be suitable for outdoor use; use

stoneware or vitreous glass. Cut into strips for easy lines or soak them off the mesh.

4 Mix up the cement-based adhesive with a small amount of black stain to make a smooth paste and trowel it directly on to the surface of the block, no more than 5mm (¼in) thick. Place a tile on the surface of the cement mixture and tap it down sharply, once only, with your mosaic nippers. Do not adjust the tile too much or will lose its strength.

5 Continue working on the design. Avoid making any sharp edges as these will have to be filed down afterwards. Make the curved line at the bottom of the seat all one

dark shade to give the design visual clarity. Place the broken slate on the cement around the square base of the seat and tap down with the mosaic nippers.

6 In between the gaps on the square base of the seat, place glass baubles, silver and glass circles, blue and white cut tiles or stones in the pattern of running water. Leave to dry completely. Grout the seat with a mixture of sand, cement and black stain. Allow to dry slowly but thoroughly. To secure the seat in position, use a mortar of sand and cement to attach the uni garden stool to an existing sound surface, or dig out a shallow base for two high-density blocks and attach.

garden ornament

Only the most minimalist of gardeners wishes to exclude any suggestion of ornament from their garden. The rest of us like to add decorative touches to personalize the space. Containers, in particular, are an ideal choice for mosaic and provide a splash of colour in the garden.

pots and containers

Mosaic can be applied to many kinds of containers, from night lights, window boxes and chimney pots to the largest urn. The most commonly covered pots are terracotta. There is also a wide range of excellent plastic containers available that accurately replicate almost any kind of finish you care to name, from terracotta, verdigris and copper to stone; mosaic can be applied to add detail and personalize these standard pots. Use a frost-resistant terracotta pot as a base where you can, and if it is not glazed you must varnish the inside to stop moisture seeping through from the inside and pushing off the tesserae. This is important if the pot is to be used for plants that are left outside. It is also best to use water- and frost-resistant cements and grouts.

Considerations to take into account concern not only the appearance of the container, but the plants as well. Ensure that your design and the colour palette complement the environment, for example, a restrained geometric design would suit a clipped topiary box tree, but a more vibrant, abstract design would harmonize with bright red geraniums.

An elaborately carved or shaped antique-style container, in real or simulated stone, may need a different treatment. Large urns look good partially covered with mosaic as it highlights the contrast between the pot and mosaic, but try to use tesserae that enhance the base colour. Urns make stunning focal points and add a sculptural feel to any garden.

birdbaths and ponds

In a birdbath, the contrast between the colours of mosaic and the glistening water makes for endless fascination. A simple

below **A bright urn and birdbath with strong colours and designs, ideal for dark or shady courtyards.**

left A traditional garden urn decorated with an unusual modern face.

below left This garden planter, by Celia Gregory, was made using bricks, shaped with cement and covered with smashed royal blue ceramic tiles. Stones decorate the top.

below right In a predominantly green space, brightly patterned ceramic pots by Cleo Mussi add interest.

design is best here, but, you might like to include some metallic or mirrored tesserae to increase the twinkling of light, an effect that provides the visual equivalent of the sound of gently splashing water. This lively effect may not be so powerful in the small confines of a birdbath, but the movement of the water and the fluttering of drinking and bathing birds adds immeasurably to a feeling of life and vitality.

Shallow troughs and ponds will also attract wildlife and are good subjects to cover with mosaic as you will still be able to see the design through the water.

mosaic and water

Water features have played an important role in design for centuries. In many cultures, water has a symbolic and philosophical meaning. Islamic garden designers have incorporated flowing water into gardens for generations: for them, it is not only beautiful and cooling in hot, dry climates, it also carries an association of cleansing and purity.

With the natural affinity between mosaic and water, fountains and other water features are an ideal opportunity for the mosaicist to display skill and imagination. The robustness and strength of colour of mosaic is an effective counterbalance to the clear, fleeting nature of water. Mosaic can be varied to suit any setting, its resistance to water means rain or fountains cannot harm it or dim its vibrancy, and the play of ever-changing outdoor light adds constant interest.

above right Circles of oblong mosaics in blues and sea greens grow darker toward the centre of this pond by Trevor Caley, creating an illusion of depth, while random gold splashes add intriguing glitter.

right An elegant mirrored fountain by Rebecca Newnham.

opposite For richness, nothing beats gold, whether on its own or as part of a design for a bowl. A collection of water features by Elaine M. Goodwin.

It is best to keep any water feature in proportion. In a small courtyard, it can be tucked into a corner or mounted on a wall – it can even be set in a container if space is really limited.

For a natural look, a mosaic of shells, stone or pebble can form a subtle framework for a pool or fountain, which darkens and gleams where the water moistens the stones. In a formal garden, you might choose to line the floor or the edge of a pool or pond with a suitable motif. Or, in an urban garden, a square or rectangular feature with geometric decoration always looks good. In a cool, green or white garden, you might like to install a mirror, silver, gold or copper leaf fountain or birdbath so that it gleams out and creates delicate dappled reflections.

sculptural mosaics

the human form

A successful mosaic takes the simple outline of whatever it is to represent, working to the strong sweeping lines of the form. A sculptural figure, because of its three-dimensional nature, can show movement, and decorating its surface with mosaic is a highly successful partnership. Mosaic sculpture is well placed outside where you can experiment with the play of the constantly changing light.

When making your own models, the underlying construction of the object suggests the contours and the mosaic is then applied in order to enhance the figure and add the detail. Mosaic is like a skin, creating the eyes, ears, nose and mouth and the moulding of the limbs and torso.

Unless you are an expert, keep the basic structure manageable. Mosaic is not like a piece of fabric that can be stretched, so keep to a shape that lends itself to the application of mosaic: ensure that the lines and contours are large enough to have tesserae laid on them and make sure that the foundation is strong enough to carry the weight of mosaic. Many artists use the direct method to cover sculptural figures with vitreous glass, broken household tiles, smashed crockery and recycled objects, incorporating more unusual materials in details. The pieces are quite light and cover curves well. The resulting surfaces can have a robust, textural feel.

contrasting styles

Life-size mosaic figures are impressive. They have great presence when they are grouped together and can look very imposing. There is great opportunity for self-expression when combining mosaic and sculptural portraiture. You do not have to stick within the confines of skin tones and realistic-looking features. Some artists have created large-scale fantastical figures, such as Niki de Saint Phalle's tarot figures featuring glass, ceramic and mirror. In contrast, Nek Chand Saini created a park full of small mosaic figures and animals called the Rock Garden, in Chandigarh, northern India, during the 1960s. He used mainly rocks for the basic structure and recycled materials and urban rubbish to cover them.

above and below right
Cleo Mussi's group of figures are painstakingly composed of oblong mosaic pieces in grid and herringbone patterns. The heads and faces use broken crocks and cup or jug handles for ears.

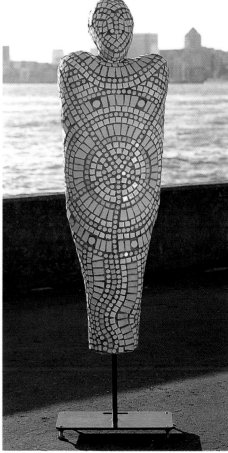

above This large mirror mosaiced installation by Celia Gregory has a metallic quality, and the three-dimensional surfaces constantly catch the light and colours in the surrounding area.

top Egyptian mummy meets tailor's dummy in this piece by Norma Vondee.

figures

above The face of this mannequin by Celia Gregory is eerie, but yet appears incredibly lifelike.

sculptural head

In this piece, mosaic adds intense colour to a three-dimensional object. Colour is used to give the two sides of the face a contrasting effect with the intense dark blues of the left-hand side balanced by the lighter blue tiles on the right-hand side, and the bright orange and lime green of the eyebrow. The colours and laying techniques convey an intensity of expression as well as a striking aesthetic effect.

materials and equipment

- **plaster head**
- **fine aluminium mesh**
- **wire**
- **cement-based adhesive**
- **small plasterer's trowel**
- **vitreous glass mosaic tiles**
- **mosaic nippers**
- **protective rubber gloves**
- **black grout**
- **tiler's sponge**
- **small screwdriver**
- **fine wet-and-dry paper**
- **cloth**

left A regal-looking head made with glass tiles.

1 In this example, the base has been made from an original plaster head. Press a fine aluminium mesh against the surface of a plaster head and fold and mould it to create the contours of the face and head. Do this in two halves, from the front and from the back, then join them together with twists of wire.

2 Create the form by applying a 12mm (½in) thick layer of cement-based adhesive over the mesh head with a small plasterer's trowel. Apply a thin layer first and work into the surface of the mesh, followed immediately (that is before it dries out) with a thicker layer. Some further modelling can be done at this stage using the build-up of adhesive to refine the contours.

3 Cover the head in quarter-cut vitreous glass mosaic pieces, sticking them to the cement base with a thin layer of cement-based adhesive. Apply this to small areas at a time with a small plasterer's trowel. The eyebrows would be a good place to start as their curving lines generate the undulating lines of the forehead.

▷

sculptural head

4 The eyes are very important in giving the piece definition and character and need to be tackled early in the process as they will generate the laying lines of the cheeks. To maintain the even flow of mosaic, try to use full-quarter tiles where possible and avoid resorting to very small pieces, which will look clumsy and be difficult to fix firmly.

5 Where you are forming a sudden change in plane, such as over the eyebrows, around the top of the crown and at the edge of the ears, try to fix the pieces so that one bevelled edge joins up to another. This will keep the joint width as narrow as possible. These pieces will slightly overhang the base and it is important to use enough adhesive to bond them firmly.

6 The lines of mosaic around the circumference of the neck have been carefully merged with the lines across the cheeks. Junctions of smaller cut tiles can be made where the line created relates to the form, as around the eye socket and abutting the ear, but where the form requires a more gradual transition a blending of the lines will be less distracting and neater.

7 Cover the neck and face in a series of three-colour mixes that blend into each other by carrying one colour over into the next mix and avoiding harsh dividing lines. Lay the hair, crown and dress in two-colour stripes; the more organized patterns help to suggest a different texture from the areas of "skin". Make a contrast between the uniform treatment of the dress and crown across the piece and the asymmetry of the face and hair.

8 When the piece is covered and the adhesive is dry, grout it wearing gloves for protection. Work the grout into the joints, curves and awkward corners with your fingers. Black grout gives extra intensity to the colours.

9 While the grout is still wet, wipe it clean using a densely textured tiler's sponge. Rinse the sponge often and avoid passing a dirty side back over the mosaic as this will spread the grout rather than clean it. In fiddly areas, you may need to scrape away excess grout with a small screwdriver. Rub down any sharp edges with fine wet-and-dry paper, then polish the piece with a cloth when dry.

animal forms

Sculptures of animals and birds do not have to be large, imposing constructions. The scale often works better when it is less intimidating and reflects their natural size. Cats, dogs, birds and other animals can be given three-dimensional depth and individual characteristics when sculpted and covered in mosaic. Fish, lizards and other reptiles are very good subjects as mosaic appears like scales or thick skin.

below left A heron made from glass, tiles, shells and stones found on the banks of the River Thames, is sited there in the shadow of Tower Bridge.

below right A slender cat, by Cleo Mussi, in white mosaic tiles has overtones of Egyptian art.

Mosaic sculptures of animals and birds work well in homes and gardens. Halls and hearths are good locations for indoor sculptures. Many people find immense pleasure in seeking out just the right piece to suit the spirit and style of their garden.

capturing the essence

You do not need to confine yourself to to realistic interpretation. Take the example of the cat: the basic sculpture provides the outline of the cat's head, body, paws and tail. The mosaic turns the shape into an identifiable animal by adding in the detail. It shows the nose, eyes and ears; shaped pieces follow the contours of the animal's body; careful selection and cutting of shaded pieces hint at the markings of fur throughout and tiny pieces hint at claws and whiskers, but the overall effect is graphic and ornamental.

The photographs on these pages show how it is possible to convey the essence of the animal while allowing your own imagination to work as well: the octopus on the right is realistically-shaped but the colours and beads used in its decoration bear little relation to its natural colouring.

garden sculptures

Animal sculptures sit comfortably amongst foliage in a garden. You could have mosaic lizards or geckos running up a garden wall or colourful butterflies on thin metal stands; frogs or fish in a pond, or birds drinking from a mosaic water fountain. If you make a shell and pebble grotto with a small rock pool, you could incorporate ornamental marine life sculptures such as sea horses, star fish and an octopus. If you have a cottage or herb garden, snails or ladybirds (bugs) would add colour and be appropriate subjects.

above This exquisite frog by Martin Cheek seems to be leaping out from the water, leaving a trail in its wake. It is made of glass mosaic with random holes through which the light shines.

right A reptile by Gaudí at the entrance of the Parc Güell, in Barcelona.

far right A mosaic octopus clinging to a rock by Takako Shimizu. Its body is decorated with beads and it is sited near water for dramatic effect.

shapes and abstracts

We have looked at different representational styles for sculptural mosaic, but some mosaic artists have explored the potential of the medium by working with more abstract shapes. Whether the pieces are small or large, their impact often lies in a combination of a strong, simple line, careful choice of materials and the fall of light on the mosaic.

Abstract mosaic sculptures in indoor and exterior living spaces can be very striking. The mirrored tusk featured opposite catches the light wonderfully and would make a good focal point in many gardens, especially in a lightly-planted contemporary space. There are many ways to create such a solid structure, and also all sorts of brilliant items available to mosaic straight on to. A smooth surface will ensure a quality mosaic finish.

construction

Brick, breezeblocks (cinderblocks) or chicken wire can be used for making the the structure and filling of abstract shapes. Fine forms may need to have a welded metalwork structure. This framework can be covered in fibreglass or meshing soaked in PVA (white) glue and then coated with a layer of adhesive. Cement and plaster are good materials for coating the forms to make a smooth surface.

above **Water collects in this eye-shaped mosaic by Norma Vondee, designed as a decorative feature for a docklands balcony.**

right **A pure white mosaic water lily by Rebecca Newnham. Its moulding allows the fall of light to emphasize the rounded shape.**

opposite **A superb sculptured horn made with thousands of rectangular mirror tiles by Rebecca Newnham.**

candle sconce

This candle sconce looks beautiful hung on a bathroom wall or in the bedroom. The mirror reflects the candlelight and, together with the small pieces of coloured tile, gives the mosaic a magical quality. Mosaic works very well on three-dimensional surfaces. This design can be modified to make a soap dish, or the sculpting techniques can be used on a larger scale.

materials and equipment

- tape measure
- plywood, 18mm (¾in) thick
- pencil, ruler and eraser
- vitreous glass tiles
- clamps
- jigsaw
- abrasive paper
- wire cutters or pliers
- chicken wire
- hammer
- **U-shaped nails**
- thick rubber gloves
- picture hooks
- bonding plaster
- mixing bowl/bucket
- **PVA** (white) glue
- sponge

- mosaic tile nippers
- pieces of mirror, stained glass, collected washed glass and amethyst (semi-precious stone)
- knife
- ready-mixed white tile adhesive
- craft (utility) knife
- small-headed screwdriver
- white grout
- dry cloths
- old sheet
- picture fixture
- screwgun
- small screws

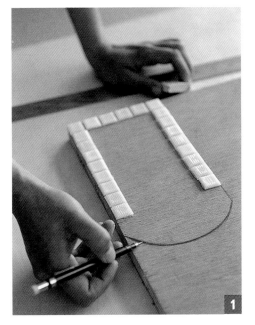

left This candle sconce holds an individual night-light, and the glimmering quality of the tiles looks enchanting.

1 Measure and mark out the plywood to a width to fit six whole glass tiles (13cm/5¼in) and length to fit ten whole tiles (22cm/9in). Use a ruler working from the corner of the wood and the two straight edges. At the end of this rectangle, draw a semicircle.

2 Clamp the wood on to the edge of a work bench. Using a jigsaw, cut out the shape. Sand the edges of the wood lightly.

3 Using wire cutters, cut out a piece of chicken wire 20 x 50cm (8 x 20in). With a hammer and U-shaped nails, attach one end of the wire to the semicircle, to create a curve.

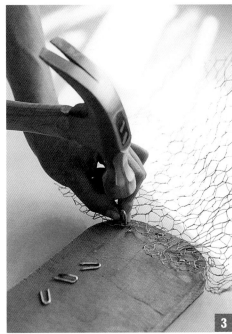

candle sconce

7 Select and clip the mosaic tiles with the tile nippers – vitreous glass, mirror, washed glass, stained glass – into small pieces. Using a knife, apply an even layer of tile adhesive to the outer edges or borders of the candle sconce. Stick strips of whole vitreous glass tiles (paper-backing side up) on to the top of the sconce, clipping the last tile to fit and meet the curve at the top of the sculptured holder.

8 Stick down strips of whole tiles, paper-backing side up, on to the sides of the sconce continuing around the base of the sculptured candleholder. Starting from the top, within the border created from whole tiles, apply adhesive and place small, clipped pieces of white tile next to the whole tiles. As the space fills, introduce light pieces of pale blue and green washed glass, working downwards. On the sculptured holder, work with richer greens and blues, and include treasures of stained glass and amethyst. Place pieces of mirror randomly to reflect the light.

4 Remove the excess wire using wire cutters or pliers. Wearing thick rubber gloves, fold the wire over and compress it to create the basic shape, fixing the top end to the wood with picture hooks.

5 Mix up some bonding plaster in a bucket into a soft but firm consistency. Pack this into the chicken wire until the structure is filled. Start to create the shape by applying small lumps to the uneven dips in the curve. Dip your fingers into water and run them over the surfaces until there is a smooth finish. Leave the plaster to dry for 24 hours.

6 Mix up PVA (white) glue and water to a ratio of one part PVA glue to five parts water. Dip a sponge in the PVA/water mix and seal the surface of the plaster with a thin film.

9 When the mosaic is finished, remove the brown paper on the whole tiles, having moistened it with a damp sponge. Clean the surfaces of the tiles and remove any excess adhesive between the gaps with a craft (utility) knife or small screwdriver.

10 Mix up powdered white grout with water, following the manufacturer's instructions. Wearing rubber gloves, apply the grout over the mosaic with your fingers. Gently clean off any excess grout with a damp sponge. After approximately ten minutes, use a dry cloth to rub away any excess grout; if the timing is right, the grout will rub off easily. Leave to dry.

11 Place the completed candle sconce on an old sheet. Mark with a pencil the area to be gouged out. Make a hole with a hammer and small-headed screwdriver. Place the picture fixture over the hole and fix in the two small screws with a screwgun.

right This method of making small sculptures with mesh can be used as the basis for many items.

mosaic techniques

planning projects

Creating a design is fun, and the references collected in your scrapbook will be very useful for inspiring your projects. The concept will affect your choice of arrangement, colours and style and there are also practical and technical decisions that need to be considered when planning a project.

below left **Drawing utensils include soft pencils, black marker pens, a ruler, eraser and special instruments, such as a protractor and right-angled ruler.**

below right **It is useful to make a simple line drawing first using a soft pencil, then emphasizing the lines with a black pen and shading in the colours to be mosaiced.**

Take inspiration for your designs from books, magazines, other artists, nature or any source that stimulates you. Keep any pictures or images that grab your attention for reference later. Stick them in a scrapbook and make notes about what you liked.

drawings

The initial drawing will be only a guide-line for your mosaic. Keep your drawing simple and clear with strong lines. If you cannot draw, trace an image or cut out a photocopy, and enlarge or adjust it to a suitable size and draw around it. You may prefer to work by completing the ideas on paper and choosing a site accordingly. When you begin to apply the tesserae, your ideas may change. This is part of the process of responding to the materials and their colour and texture.

It is not usually necessary to make all the design decisions at the beginning of the project. Creativity is a journey; allow the space during the process for new ideas and additions to unfold. When thinking about your design, bear in mind the colours, textures and contrast of the materials. Bear in mind how much time you want to spend on your mosaic, as this may influence the intricacy and complexity of the design.

starting out

If the task is site specific, make an accurate template with graph paper or brown paper and/or take measurements before you start the detailed planning and work. Make clear notes while you are on site so it is easy to decipher the figures and information gathered.

If you are a beginner, it is best to start with basic techniques. Choose a small project as a trial piece, such as a pot stand, terracotta pot for the garden or a small wall panel. But, as you become more confident, you can be more ambitious and explore your creativity.

above There is a huge range of mosaic tiles to choose from. Vitreous glass tiles shown here are best suited to indoor work.

left Tile sample boards are a useful way of choosing colours and tiles for a project. Tile suppliers have a wealth of knowledge and it is important to check that the tiles you choose suit the project you are undertaking.

choosing tiles

The appearance of the mosaic is totally dependent on the materials you use. The design may even revolve around using a certain tile, the unique quality of that material being the source of inspiration. Discovering how different materials work alone and with each other is an exciting aspect of mosaic artistry and takes time to master.

There is a fantastic range of tiles from all over the world in different colours, glazes and textures. You can use stone with its soft colours or choose from a lavish range of stained glass. There is certainly no shortage of choice. Aside from your own aesthetic decisions there are various factors to take into account when making your choice. The cost could be a consideration; for example, marble is a beautiful and durable material but it is very expensive. Porcelain offers a much cheaper alternative.

qualities of tiles

You want the mosaic to last yet some tiles are not suitable for all situations. Glass tiles or stained glass would be damaged quickly if positioned on a floor and exposed to high heels. Glazes come in varying hardnesses; a soft glaze would restrict the tile use to inside. A harder glaze can be used on the floor, and a frost-proof tile can be used outside. The fired clay that lies under the glaze also has its own individual qualities, such as absorbency, which can affect whether the tiles can go in a shower or bathroom. Each tile and material varies; it is important to check their qualities and uses with the supplier when you buy them.

choosing the right technique

Each project is different and no task is approached in exactly the same way. You need to decide what technique to use and the suitable fixing agents that are required. Here are some questions you will need to ask yourself:

- Where is the piece to be finally positioned?
- Will you work directly, for example on to the pot?
- Will you choose an indirect method, for example on to meshing, which is good for a floor panel?

- Is the site accessible – is it easier to make the mosaic off-site?
- How durable does the mosaic need to be?
- Does the mosaic need to be water-resistant, waterproof, weather- or frost-proof?

creating a workspace

A small item, such as a terracotta pot, can be decorated with mosaic in a spare room or kitchen, but mosaic fragments are sharp, and the cement and grout are dusty, so this environment is not ideal. It is advisable to allocate a special area in which to work, giving you a clean area for drawing and another space with a workbench or table for doing the mosaic.

The work place is your own creative environment so allocate wall space to hang finished mosaics and images that will inspire you. Create shelving to store books and files as an organized work area allows space for ideas to blossom.

posture

The most comfortable way to mosaic is definitely working at an easel or a table. It is important to have the seat or stool at a suitable height. It is worth spending time getting this right so that a good posture can be maintained and you can avoid aches in the shoulders and back.

large mosaics

When working on a mosaic that is too big for a table or easel, it is necessary to work on or at least prepare the design on the floor. A hard surface is required to work on, so create this using a large piece of wood. If you are using an indirect technique, such as meshing or brown paper, draw up the design and get a clear understanding of the whole image. Then you can cut the image into fragments and work in sections on the workbench.

If you need to see the whole design develop, work on the floor and protect the surrounding surfaces with plastic sheeting. This can be hard on the back, so you must take regular breaks and have a good stretch.

a tidy workspace

Once you have chosen where and how to work and what to mosaic, gather all the required materials, such as mosaic tile nippers and tools, together, mix enough fixing agents and prepare a good range of tiles before commencing.

Keep the work area clean, sweeping away loose fragments regularly. It also makes good sense to keep coloured tiles in

right Good light, a work surface and seating at the right height for good posture are essential for comfortable mosaic making.

some kind of order, placing different tiles, colours and shapes in separate small piles. When working with adhesive, clean off any excess while it is damp; if left overnight the cement will harden and become very difficult to remove. Sweep up or vacuum at the end of each session, as fragments get everywhere and can be sharp. Cleaning and reorganizing will make the next day's work much easier.

left Larger projects can be planned on the floor or in an area where it is possible to see the whole design.

water

You will need access to water. Do not get different cement and grouts into the drains as serious blockages will occur. When cleaning mixing bowls, always throw away as much excess as possible. It is advisable to place gauze over the plug, otherwise clean the drains regularly.

lighting

Ideally, position the table near a natural source of light. Daylight is the best way to see true colour. When light is limited or when you are working at night, use daylight bulbs. It is best to have more than one light source to avoid shadows.

storage

When organizing materials, it is a good idea to build shelving and store tiles in glass or clear plastic jars so it is easy to see what there is in stock and the colours. Tools are expensive and rust easily, so keep them clean and dry. Adhesives and grouts solidify if they get wet, so they must all be stored in a damp-free area, preferably in sealed containers. Most chemicals have a limited shelf life and can go off, so check the contents regularly.

safety

There are sensible precautions you can take to avoid injuring yourself:

- Wear goggles when cutting materials to avoid getting fragments in your eyes. Hold the mosaic tile nippers away from your face.
- Wear a face mask when cutting wood or mixing powder to avoid inhaling fine powder into sinuses and lungs.
- Wear hardwearing gloves when cutting wire and use rubber or latex gloves when mixing up powders, and also when grouting, cleaning or sculpting. Your hands will get dry and sore if they come into contact with water and adhesives for too long. It is also recommended to wear thin latex gloves when making mosaics. Take care and keep antiseptic cream, plasters and hand cream handy!
- Hold mosaic tile nippers at the far end of the handle to avoid hand blisters.
- Always clean and vacuum the work area regularly to avoid an unnecessary build-up of dust.
- Create your mosaic with awareness to the safety of those around you, as well as yourself.

preparing materials

A mosaic is an image or design made up of cut-up fragments of tiles or a variety of different materials. It is therefore necessary to prepare materials in various ways before they are ready to mosaic with. Mosaic tile nippers are used to cut shapes from most materials. A hammer and hardie are used for hard and thick materials such as marble or smalti.

far right Tiles soaked in warm water will easily slip off the brown paper backing.

Prepare and clip the materials you will be using before you start to mosaic, as a painter would mix a palette of paints. This will leave you free to concentrate on the laying of the mosaic design.

sheet mosaic

Many mosaic tiles come on sheets, either on fibreglass meshing or on brown paper; the tiles are about 2cm (¾in) square and the sheets are approximately 30cm (12in) square. These are useful for laying a large

area. On smaller mosaics, when working with the tesserae-style shapes, you should remove the tiles from the backing.

To remove tiles from sheets formed with brown paper or meshing, soak the whole sheets in clean warm water. When the glue has dissolved the tiles will slip off easily.

smashed ceramic tiles

Gaudí is famous for his extensive use of mosaic in his fairytale buildings in Barcelona. They are very colourful and predominantly use ceramic tiles smashed into small fragments. Ceramic tiles come in an enormous range of colours, tones, textures and glazes, and are suitable for both interior and exterior use as many are frost-proof. They are fun and easy to work with.

smashed ceramic tiles

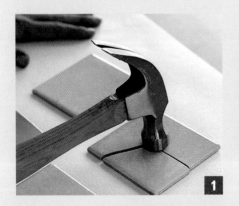

1 Wearing goggles and gloves, smash the tiles with a small hammer, aiming at the centre of the tile. To make these fragments smaller, gently smash with a hammer in the centre of the fragment.

2 Pieces can fly all over the place if you hit the tile too hard, so for protection, you can cover the tiles with a cloth. Use the mosaic nippers to shape the ceramics into the size and style required.

far left Glass and mirror can be cut with a glass cutter: score the surface lightly, using a ruler as a guide, then break.

left A hammer and hardie are used to break thick materials such as marble and smalti into pieces.

clipping tiles

Mosaic tile nippers are the essential tool for any mosaicist, and are good for clipping many materials, from ceramic to washed glass.

With practice it is possible to cut intricate shapes. Hold the mosaic nippers at the end of the handles for the best possible leverage. Place the rounded side of the head over the tile, which need only be inserted a few millimetres. To cut the tile in half, position the mosaic tile nippers in the centre of the tile and ensure that the head is pointing in the direction the cut is needed. Stabilize the tile by holding the opposite edge between the thumb, forefinger and index finger. Press the ends of the handles together.

Always wear goggles as initially the tiles seem to fly all over the place. As the hand muscles strengthen and the correct pressure is applied, it becomes possible to control the cuts, and the fingers support the bits in place. If the cut goes astray, nibble away the excess with little clips on the edge of the tile.

tile cutter and tile saw

The hand tile cutter is used for traditional tiling and is available from do-it-yourself stores. It will cut straight lines, although its use is limited to ceramic tiles with a soft clay base. Hard floor tiles or stone need to be cut with a wet tile saw, which is a specialized piece of equipment but is essential for certain tasks, such as cutting thin strips of marble, which are then made into the correct size for mosaicing with a hammer and hardie. It is possible to hire these. The saw cuts the material with a metal disc that is revolved by a motor and kept cool with water. As the tile hits the blade, the water can spray outward, making this quite a messy but effective technique. Wear protective clothing.

glass cutter

This is used for cutting straight lines or large shapes in stained glass and mirror. Score the surface lightly with the cutter, then use the ball of the cutter to tap the underside gently; it will crack along the line. Be careful and wear goggles and gloves when handling glass and mirror, since even the smallest splinters are sharp and cut easily. Tile nippers are good for making smaller cuts and detailed shapes.

hammer and hardie

These are the traditional tools for cutting stone and smalti; both these materials are too thick for modern tile clippers. Hold the material over the chisel between the thumb and forefinger and swing the hammer down on to this point. With practice, accurate cutting is obtained.

right, from the top
Tile cutters, which are good for cutting straight lines; a tile scorer; mosaic tile nippers, the essential mosaic tool for cutting tiles into shapes; a utility knife; and a glass cutter for cutting stained glass and mirror.

preparing surfaces

Mosaics can be laid on to a variety of different surfaces and, as long as the correct procedures are followed, they will be hardwearing and waterproof. Traditional mosaics were laid on to a cement bed. Now, we can also mosaic on to all sorts of different surfaces: wood, old furniture, plaster, ceramic, terracotta or fibreglass. This versatility gives many interesting opportunities for today's mosaicists.

bases

Unless working with a sculptured form, you should work on to a flat, even surface for a professional quality mosaic. Sand down uneven surfaces, or if working on to cement, a new surface could be laid; self-levelling cement is an easy option.

The base or surface should be rigid. For example, floorboards are flexible and the mosaic will lift if there is movement. It is necessary to lay a thin layer of wood, cut to fit and screwed in evenly over the entire surface. This will provide a suitable working surface. Wood is very good to mosaic on to; however, if the mosaic is going outside or if it is to come into contact with water, make sure you use wood that is exterior grade, such as marine ply.

priming surfaces

Most working surfaces, such as wood, concrete, terracotta urns, old furniture or plaster, are porous, therefore you must seal the surface. Sealing or priming the surface greatly improves the sticking power of adhesive and makes the final mosaic more hardwearing and waterproof. Before sealing, it is important to ensure that the surface is clean of all loose debris and hair.

Smooth surfaces, such as wood or fine plaster, should be scored. On more slippery surfaces, such as plastics or existing tiles, a special two-part resin primer can be brushed on to provide a key. It creates a surface that adhesive can easily attach to.

To improve the grip on surfaces that cannot be scored, such as terracotta, mix a small amount of cement-based adhesive powder with water into a runny, creamy consistency and brush a thin film on to the surface. Allow it to dry for 24 hours.

priming wood

1 Take a craft (utility) knife and score the surface of the wood, creating a key. This improves the grip between the tiles and the adhesive.

2 Mix up PVA (white) glue with water in a ratio of one part glue to five parts water. Apply this evenly with a dense sponge.

fixing tiles

Once the surface has been properly prepared there are various ways to fix the tiles. Choosing which technique is used depends partly on where the mosaic is situated and partly on personal preference. Direct methods involve placing the material straight on to the working surfaces. The indirect techniques involve working on to meshing or paper off-site and fitting the mosaic later.

below You will need some, if not all the tools below, to prepare surfaces and apply cement. Clockwise from top left: a hard bristle brush, a paintbrush for glue, a notched trowel, a hammer, a chisel, a palette knife, dustpan and brush, a rubber squeegee and a cement and adhesive applicator.

Mosaic was traditionally laid into a bed of cement and the remains of ancient artworks still exist in good condition. Mosaics were built to last. Traditional stone and smalti have a depth that allows the tesserae to sit in the mortar, while modern materials are often much thinner and need to stick as well as be embedded.

cement-based adhesives

There is an vast range of modern cement-based adhesives for use on both direct and indirect mosaics. They come in a variety of shades, mainly white and grey. Your choice of colour will be influenced by what colour you want to grout in. Choose grey if planning to grout with grey, black or dark colours, and white for lighter shades.

Medium-strength adhesive comes in tubs ready-mixed, which is fine for decorative pieces or if the mosaic does not need to be particularly waterproof. Most large tile companies have their recommended range of powder-based adhesive and additives. It is always worth asking what materials most suit the job you are undertaking. They will have a variety of products for all situations, from exterior frost-proof, cement-based adhesives through to flexible liquid additives that can be added for extra protection against movement or to make the adhesive suitable for a shower.

epoxy resin

This is a strong glue made up of two separate components: the hardener and the resin. The resin is good for using in underwater locations or in damp places. However, it has a limited working time and it is sticky and toxic, so wear a mask. Use epoxy resin when working with the direct method.

direct method

This is good for working on to wood or sculptured forms, when working with smashed ceramic tiles, washed glass, tiles of different heights, or when covering large areas. It is also good to work directly into cement because it avoids having to spend additional time fitting and allows the design to develop in the environment where the mosaic is situated.

Direct methods are easier techniques to start with and recommended for beginners. Master these first; the skills will then help you when using the indirect techniques. PVA (white) glue is good for sticking tiles directly on to wood; use it undiluted or mixed with a small amount of water to make it easier to apply. PVA glue is water-based so its use is limited to decorative items that do not need to be hardwearing or go outside. Quick-set adhesives dry in four hours, so drying time is drastically reduced.

choosing your technique

The direct method of mosaic is a satisfying and traditional technique, yet in some situations it is just not practical. It can get messy; adhesive gets on to your hands and then on to the tiles, so clean your hands and the tiles regularly.

Using this method can also be uncomfortable, for example when you are trying to fit tiles behind a toilet, when you are stretching on a ladder to reach the top corner of a wall. And the perfect tile dropping into a mess of clipped tiles is annoying. Learning to use indirect methods will help avoid these situations.

working with adhesive

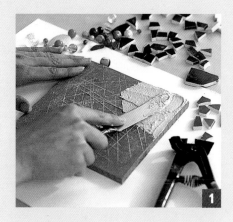 

1 Mix white powder adhesive with water in the ratio of 2½ parts powder to 1 part water, until you have a smooth consistency. Choose and prepare the tiles you are going to use. Apply adhesive to the panel with a knife.

2 Stick the tiles into the adhesive ensuring good contact by pushing the tile in with your fingertips. Use too much adhesive and the excess will squeeze through the gaps between the tiles and it will get messy. Use too little and the tiles fall off.

working with PVA glue

   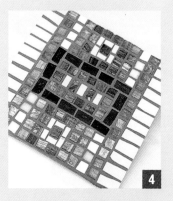

1 Cut a piece of wood 15 x 15cm (6 x 6in); it is not necessary to seal the panel first. Choose a selection of tiles. Clip the tiles into a selection of quarters and halves. Have a play around with the tiles; mosaic does not have to be complicated to look good.

2 Once you are happy with the arrangement of tiles, use a small brush to apply the PVA (white) glue to the back of the tiles. Stick them on to the panel. The glue does not dry instantly so they will move around at first. Leave the tiles to dry for several hours.

3 Once the glue is dry, it is time for grouting. Mix up some grey powder adhesive with water in the ratio of 3½ parts grout to 1 part water. Apply with a squeegee or your fingertips, then wipe down the surface with a damp sponge. Once it is dry, polish up the tiles.

4 This design works with simple lines, and the different types of tile bring depth and contrast. The square of black vitreous glass is balanced by the smaller squares and white lines and contrasted by the matt cream porcelain halves. Richness is created with the shimmering bronzed pink tile.

indirect method

Ultimately, the mosaic will be embedded into adhesive cement, but there are circumstances when the work cannot be done directly. Perhaps the mosaic is situated in a location that is awkward to reach, such as behind a sink or on a ceiling. If the mosaic is sited outside or in a public place it is liable to get damaged during work in progress. Maybe the mosaic is intricate and will take months to finish. In these cases it makes sense to complete the mosaic in the comfort of the studio and fit the whole piece in one go.

brown paper method

This reverse technique is very useful to learn. It is used when it is essential to have a very smooth mosaic. When using this technique, the tiles are laid face down on brown paper or mesh; if the tiles are uneven in any way the irregularity will occur on the underside of the tile. It is also good if the completed mosaic needs to be fitted directly into cement, for example in a swimming pool.

The method's use is limited to tessera where the colour runs over the entire tile, as the design is worked in reverse. (This can take some time to get your head around, especially when using graphics.) The side that will be seen is stuck on to the paper, so if the colour is not visible it is impossible to see the design.

The benefit of this method is that the finished sheets of mosaic can be cut up and transported easily. Fitting, however, is time-consuming and fiddly as the brown paper needs to be soaked off with warm water to reveal the mosaic underneath.

meshing method

Fine weave fibre meshing acts as a perfect base for a mosaic. The tiles are fixed directly on to the meshing with glue, so it is possible to see the mosaic design developing and taking shape, but it is an indirect method. Large areas can be cut up and transported easily. Fitting is much less laborious than the reverse brown paper technique.

above The completed indirect mosaic needs to be cut into sections that can be handled easily.

below left This soft mesh is used for subtle relief work. Chicken wire is more effective for larger scale sculpting. Big exterior sculpting can be formed with bricks or breezeblocks (cinderblocks) then covered with a layer of cement.

below right Glue the mosaic pieces straight on to the fibreglass mesh.

grouting

Grouting is incredibly satisfying; the mosaic becomes unified and the images and colours blend. Designs that feel garish or too busy before grouting are softened, patterns that work with movement come to life and three-dimensional sculptures feel like they have grown a skin. Grouting completes the whole picture and can also add different effects to your work.

On a practical level, grouting is when the gaps between the tiles are filled with a cement mortar that has a different quality to the adhesives. The process strengthens the mosaic and ensures that it is waterproof. Therefore, mosaic is a functional art form that can be used in swimming pools, showers, water features, external wall murals or lavish floors.

Grout is a different colour to adhesive. It comes either ready-mixed or in a powder and in a variety of colours. There are also powdered dyes (stains) you can add to create almost any colour you want. The colour you choose will have a profound effect on the colours and look of the finished mosaic. Some of these differences can be seen in the four panels below. The grid of grey grout overpowers the white tiles and the white grout is also very strong. However, the cream grout works well with the white tile as there is balance. The beige grout warms the white tiles. White grout will blend with pale tiles,

above Wear gloves and grout your mosaic using a rubber squeegee. Rub the grout into any gaps using your fingertips.

top For grouting and cleaning your mosaics, you will need a mixing trowel, a grout spreader, some cleaning cloths, a sponge, a bowl and lots of protective plastic sheeting.

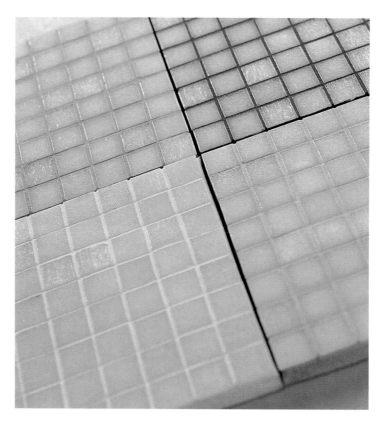

left These four panels of white vitreous glass mosaic were grouted in four different shades: clockwise from left, beige, grey, cream and white.

lighten darker colours and contrast blacks. Black grout will deepen blacks and blues, make reds and greens really rich and contrast with white. The qualities and varieties are endless, giving you great scope for creativity. Grouting is a messy job, especially if using dyes, so protect your clothes and surrounding well.

when to grout

Grout your work when the mosaic is finished and the cement-based adhesive is dry. Before grouting, small mosaics can be gently shaken to remove loose adhesive, and any loose tiles can be re-adhered. On larger-scale mosaics, light vacuuming can be effective. On a large-scale project, do not grout the whole surface in one go because you may well go to clean off the grout and find it has dried up, especially in a centrally heated bathroom! Take it one section at a time. The grout should be left to dry for 24 hours.

right Grout comes in different colours that can alter the finished look of the mosaic.

grouting and sponging

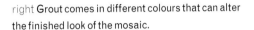

1 When making the mosaic, adhesive can squeeze through the gaps between the tiles. Scrape this away with a blade or small screwdriver or utility knife. Then ensure that the mosaic is clean and all loose debris is removed.

2 In a bowl, mix together the powdered grout and clean water, following the manufacturer's instructions.

3 Wearing rubber gloves, apply the grout over the mosaic using your fingers or a rubber squeegee. Push the paste into the gaps and evenly over the surface.

4 Wipe away any excess grout with a damp sponge. After approximately 10 minutes, the remaining grout can be rubbed away easily with a dry cloth. If you leave it for too long, the gentle rub becomes a lengthy and hard task involving wire (steel) wool and wire brushes.

finishing your work

Spending time doing a good grouting job saves time when it comes to cleaning. Theoretically, only a thin film of grout should be left behind. It is very exciting seeing the colours and the design of the mosaic being revealed as the film of grout that hides the detail is removed. The colours come alive and all the hard work suddenly feels really worthwhile.

below left **This colourful panel is lightened by the white grout, and the glazed tiles laid in Gaudí-style mosaic have a fresh flowing feel. Firstly, spray the mosaic with glass cleaner.**

below right **Polish with a clean dry cloth. The colours weave into each other, while the mirror and glass balls shimmer within the mosaic.**

Varying glazes hold the grout differently, grout comes off a shiny glaze very easily but clings to matt porcelain. It is possible to buy an acid called patio cleaner, used by builders for cleaning cement off brick-work. When diluted with warm water it is very effective for removing resilient grout. Sponge or pour this on to the mosaic and it will make a great fizzing noise as it eats away at the grout left on the surface of the tiles. After a few minutes, sponge away the dirty water. Really resistant areas can be cleaned with wire (steel) wool or scraped away with a steel blade. Polish up with dry clean cloths.

sealing

Stone and pebbles look richer when sealed, appearing as slightly wet and retaining the subtlety of the tone without adding a varnish or shine to the surface. Sealants come in matt or shiny varieties. Beeswax can be rubbed on to matt tiles giving them a deeper colour. Terracotta tiles need to be treated with linseed oil. This is flammable so always dampen cloths that the oil comes into contact with and dispose of them away from any heat source.

maintenance

The best way to maintain a mosaic is to clean it regularly. A floor mosaic should be swept and mopped down with a gentle cleaning agent, making sure excess and dirty water is removed properly. Decorative mosaics should be dusted and cleaned using glass cleaner and a dry cloth. Bathroom mosaics should be cleaned as you would any tile. Regular cleaning avoids the build-up of resilient dirt. However, if the mosaic is allowed to get really dirty use the acid cleaner. Give the mosaic a good scrub with a brush or wire wool. Acid is a strong cleaner and may well eat away at loose grout, so it may be necessary to re-grout. If the correct technical steps are taken, the mosaic could last for a millennium.

hanging

A small mosaic can be hung like a picture, using wire and picture hooks. However, hanging a larger, heavier mosaic requires more thought. It is important to see whether the wall you intend to fix the mosaic on to can hold the weight. Plasterboard will not, so if it is a partition wall find the supporting struts and fix into them. When fixing into brick or plaster it is necessary to drill holes. With a pen, mark on the wall the correct position for the fixings. Use a bit and a drill piece that is compatible with the screw size you have chosen to drill holes with. Place wall plugs in the screw holes when fixing the mosaic to the wall, and make sure the screws enter these wall plugs. Mosaic panels can be fixed to the wall with mirror plates. These are fixings that are fitted to the wood on the back of the panel and then the mirror plates are screwed on to the wall.

If you are unsure, always seek advice. It would be terrible to find your work of art shattered on the floor.

siting

There are no hard and fast rules about where to site your mosaic, it is a matter of judgement and common sense, which you must learn to trust. Get a friend or relative to hold the mosaic in place so you can have a look. When something is right it feels right. If you are unsure, swap with your helper and ask their opinion.

Aside from the positioning of the mosaic, bear in mind the colour of the surrounding walls. You do not want them to clash with each other or the colour of the wall to overpower the mosaic.

lighting

Mosaics nearly always look their best in natural light with its soft tones. Yet the night-time light is important and needs consideration. Try lighting your mosaic with a spotlight fixed on the ceiling or a traditional picture light that lights from above. Just be careful not to over-light and bleach out the colours and subtle reflective quality of the tiles. Try different colours and wattages of bulb and place the light source at different angles and distances.

above This panel has been designed to look like an antique. The image of the female bathers has been created with marble, and the soft subtle quality of the stone works well in this environment.

left Some of the tools you may need when siting and installing your mosaic. Clockwise, from top right: a saw, a hammer, abrasive paper, wire (steel) wool, U-shaped hooks, pliers, a screwdriver, picture wire, picture hooks, hanging hooks, screw eyes, screws, wall plugs and an eraser.

mosaic suppliers and artists

Making mosaics requires few specialist materials and equipment, the majority of which can be found in most do-it-yourself, craft or hardware stores. The suppliers listed here include speciality suppliers that may be useful when making the projects in this book.

Australia

Alan Patrick Pty Ltd
11 Agnes Street
Jolimont, Victoria 3002
Tel: (61) 3 9654 8288

Camden Art Centre Pty Ltd
188–200 Gertrude Street
Fitzroy, Victoria, 3065

The Crafts and Gifts Gallery
306 Hay Street
Subiaco, WA, 6088
craftgallery@optusnet.com.au
Tel: (61) 8 9381 8215
Store and mail order.

Finn's Stained Glass
129 Boundary Road
Peakhurst, NSW, 2210
www.finnglass.com.au
Tel: 1800 627 989

Glass Craft Australia
54–56 Lexton Road
Box Hill North
Victoria 3129
Tel: (61) 3 9897 4188
www.citysearch.com.au/mel/
glasscraft

Handworks Supplies Pty Ltd
244 Chappel Street
Prahan, Victoria, 3181
www.handworks.com.au
Tel: (61) 3 9533 8566

Rodda Pty Ltd
62 Beach Street
Port Melbourne
Victoria

France

Mosaik
Atelier
17, rue Foucault
92110 Clichy
Tel: 47 30 98 10
Fax: 47 30 90 30

Italy

Angelo Orsoni
Canneregio 1045
30121 Venezia
Tel: (39) 41 244 0002

Mario Dona e Figli Snc
Via Marchetti Guiseppe 6
33097 Spilimbergo (PN)
Friuli

North America

Alice's Stained Glass
7015 N. 58th Avenue
Glendale, AZ 85301
Tel: (602) 939-7260

Brian's Crafts Unlimited
PO Box 731046
Ormond Beach
FL 32173-046
Tel: (904) 672-2726

Deco Tile
362 Davenport Road
Toronto
Canada M5R 1K6
Tel: (416) 413 7985

Dick Blick
PO Box 1267
Galesburg, IL 61402
Tel: (309) 343-6181

Eastern Art Glass
PO Box 341
Wcykoff, NJ 07481
Tel: (201) 847-0001

Hudson Glass Co., Inc.
219 N. Division St.
Peekshill, NY 10566
Tel: (914) 737-2124

Ideal Tile of Manhatten Inc.
405 East 51st St.
New York, NY 10022
Tel: (212) 759-2339

United Kingdom

Edgar Udney and Co Ltd
314 Balham High Road
London SW17 7AA
Tel: 020 8767 8181
Ceramic, glass and smalti. Fixing materials. Mail order service.

Fired Earth
Twyford Mill
Oxford Road
Adderbury
Oxfordshire OX17 3HP
Tel: 01295 812088

James Hetley & Co
Glasshouse Fields
London E1 9JA
Tel: 020 7780 2345

Lead & Light Warehouse
35a Hartland Road
London NW1 8BD
Tel: 020 7485 0997
Stained glass. Mail order service.

Mosaic Workshop
1a Princeton Street
London W1R 4AX
Tel: 020 7404 9249
Glass, ceramic, smalti and marble. Tools and fixing materials. Mail order service.

Paul Fricker Ltd
Well Park, Willeys Avenue
Exeter
Devon EX2 8BE
Tel: 01392 278636

The Pot Company
16–20 Raymouth Road
London SE16 2DB
Tel: 020 7394 9711

Reed Harris
Riverside House
27 Carnworth Road
London SW6 3HR
Tel: 020 7736 7511
Ceramic, glass and marble. Fixing materials. Mail order service.

Tower Ceramics
91 Parkway
Camden Town
London NW1 9PP
Tel: 020 7485 7192

World's End Tiles
Silverthorne Road
London SW8 3HE
Tel: 020 7720 8358

mosaic artists

Emma Biggs
Mosaic Workshop
Unit B, 443–449 Holloway Road
London N7 6LJ
Tel: 020 7263 2997

Trevor Caley
Sunnyside Cottage
Woodgreen, Fordingbridge
Hampshire SP6 2AU

Stephen Charnock
Tatlock Farm
Asmall Lane, Ormskirk
Lancashire L39 8RA
Tel: 01695 573636

Martin Cheek Mosaics
Flint House, 21 Harbour Street
Broadstairs, Kent CT10 1ET
Tel: 01843 861958
www.martincheek.com
e-mail:martin@martincheek.com
*Mosaics made to commission and
supplier of mosaic materials and
kits. Monthly courses at Flint House.*

Celia Gregory and Martin Cohen
Enterprise House, Tudor Grove
London E9 7QL
Tel: 020 8510 9300/07939 127632
Mosaics made to commission.

Elizabeth De'Ath
4 Benson Quay
London E1 9TR
Tel: 020 7481 0389

Elaine M. Goodwin
4 Devonshire Place
Exeter EX4 6JA

Robert Grace
The Gallery of Mosaic Art and
    Design
Suite 324, Business Design Centre
52 Upper Street
London N1 0QH
Tel: 020 7288 6050
www.mosaicartanddesign.com

Scott Harrower
38 Cecil Road
Bardon, QLD, 4065
Australia
shmosaic@bigpond.com
Tel: (07) 3368 1671

Maggy Howarth
Cobblestone Designs
Hilltop, Wennington
Lancaster LA2 8NY
Tel: 01524 274264
*Pebble mosaics for private gardens
and public spaces.*

Tessa Hunkin
Mosaic Workshop
Unit B, 443–449 Holloway Road
London N7 6LJ
Tel: 020 7263 2997

Mosaik
10 Kensington Square
London W8 5EP
Tel: 020 7795 6253
Mosaics made to commission.

Cleo Mussi
Uplands Cottage
99 Slad Road
Stroud
Gloucestershire GL5 1QZ
Mosaics made to commission.

Rebecca Newnham
Palmerston
Kingston, Ringwood
Hampshire BH24 3BG

Paris Ceramics
583 Kings Road
London SW6 2EH
Tel: 020 7371 7778
www.parisceramics.com

Stephen Smith
Mozaiek Art
142 St. Peters Road
South Ham, Basingstoke
Hants RG22 6TH
Tel: 01256 844799
www.mozaiekart.co.uk

Claire Stewart
The Glass Elevator
79 London Road
Markyate, St. Albans
Hertfordshire AL3 8JP
Tel: 01582 840901
www.theglasselevator.co.uk

Steven Vella
PO Box 734
Darlinghurst, NSW, 2010
Australia
Tel: (02) 9557 9307

Norma Vondee
8 Benson Quay
London E1 9TR
Tel: 020 7481 4563
Mosaics made to commission.

Sheryl Wilson
Reptile
Unit P21, Bow Wharf
Grove Road
London E3
Tel: 07976 522013
Garden ornamental mosaics.

index

abstract patterns 32, 42–3, 122
    colour panel 78–9
accessories 106–9
adhesives 150
andamento 58
animal patterns 6, 18, 34–5, 36–7, 58
    sculptural 132–3
arabesques 14
Art Deco 52
Art Nouveau 16–17
Aztecs 15

Bahouth, Candace 18
Baird, Helen 38
Barcelona 16, 17, 55, 66, 67, 146
bathrooms 46, 51, 72, 75, 76, 90, 93,
    108, 143
beads 6, 28, 29
bedrooms 61, 76, 106, 108
benches 116
Biggs, Emma 76
birdbaths 117, 120
birds 34–5, 120
Bizzaria 24
borders 6, 11, 42, 62–3, 76, 77, 100–1
broken ceramics 17, 26, 54, 55, 60–1,
    146
brown paper 144, 149
buildings 66–7
Byzantine mosaic 12–13, 18, 23, 32,
    40, 81

cabinets 61, 108, 109
Caley, Trevor 122

calligraphy 14
candle sconce 136–9
cartoons 32
Casa Battló, Barcelona 17
Casa Miló, Barcelona 67
Celtic art 18, 42, 63, 101
ceramics 6, 18, 24, 26, 46, 60, 61, 69,
    143, 146, 147
Chagall, Marc 32
chairs 46, 107, 116
checks 7, 42, 58, 76
Cheek, Martin 33, 34, 37, 133
chequerboard 42, 55, 58
chests 108
chevrons 58
china 26, 27, 60–1
Chirico, Giorgio de 40
choosing materials 143
Christianity 12–13
circles 42, 58, 82
classical mosaic 10–11, 22, 32, 34, 35,
    40, 42, 62
clay 55, 60, 90, 101, 143
cleaning mosaics 154
cleaning workspace 144–5
Cohen, Martin 107
colour 11, 12, 14, 15, 22, 23, 42, 46
    bold effects 92
    contrasting 54–5
    hot and cool 49, 50–1
    matching 52–3
Cominitti, Anna Tabata 109
considerations 46–7, 48–9, 143
Constantinople (Istanbul) 12, 40
containers 120–1
contemporary mosaic 18, 34–5
contrasts 54–5, 82–3
copper 23, 122
creating a workspace 144–5
cubes 11, 42
Cubism 18
cutters 147

daylight 49, 50, 53, 75
    workrooms 145
De'Ath, Elizabeth 18, 101
design 6–7, 40, 46, 47, 48–9, 52, 54–5
    planning projects 142–3
    simplifying 56–7
desks 109
diamond patterns 42, 80, 92
dining rooms 49
direct method 85, 149, 150

drawings 56–7, 62, 142
dressers 108
Dumbarton Oaks, Washington DC
    82
dust masks 145

environmental issues 89
ethnic art 32
exteriors 48–9, 68–9, 82–3, 152
eye level 47, 49

Farrand, Beatrice 82
Fassett, Kaffe 18
figurative mosaics 6, 7, 10, 11, 32–3,
    58, 126–8
finishing 154–5
floors 7, 11, 24, 46, 52, 61, 90–3, 143
    bathroom 93
    exterior 82–3, 152
    snakes and ladders 84–7
flowers 38–9, 58
focal points 47
folk art 16, 38, 52
fountains 120
fresco 11
friezes 76–7
frost resistance 48, 69, 120, 143
function 46–7

gardens 47, 49, 70, 77, 82
    decoration 120–1, 132
    garden rooms 46, 61, 90
    furniture 116–7
    uni garden seat 118–19
Gaudí, Antoni 16, 17, 18, 55, 66, 133,
    146
Gellert bathhouse, Hungary 80
geometric patterns 6, 7, 11, 14, 42–3,
    49, 55, 58, 62, 76, 122
glass 6, 18, 24, 25, 28, 35, 46, 47, 55, 60,
    61, 69, 80, 90, 101, 147
    stained glass 27, 103–5, 143
glazes 143
gloves 145, 146, 147
goggles 145, 146, 147
gold 12, 15, 38, 54, 122
    gold leaf tile 18, 22–23
Goodwin, Elaine M. 18, 68, 70, 77, 92,
    101, 122
Grace, Robert 55, 72
Greek key 11, 42, 58, 62, 80, 90
Greeks, ancient 10, 22, 62
Gregory, Celia 18, 33, 47, 58, 60, 61, 63,

    70, 71, 81, 100, 103, 108, 121, 127,137
grouting 53, 152–3, 154
guilloche patterns 62

hallways 42, 46, 51, 77, 90, 132
hammer and hardie 22, 146, 147
hanging mosaics 155
Hearst, William Randolph 80
hearth, making a mosaic 94–7
home office 109
Horta, Victor 17
household tiles 26
Howarth, Maggy 35
human form 6, 10, 11, 32–3, 58
    sculpture 126–8, 129–31
Hundertwasser, Friedensreich
    66–7, 103

Incas 15
indirect method 85, 144, 149
insect patterns 34–5
interiors 48, 72–5, 90–3
Ishtar pattern 62
Isidore, Raymond 68, 69
Islam 14–15, 38, 42, 122
Istanbul (Constantinople) 12, 40
Italy 18, 23

jewellery 7, 46
jewels 29

kitchens 46, 49, 61, 76, 77, 90, 106, 144
    kitchen units 108
Klee, Paul 42
Klimt, Gustav 110
Kudo, Haruya 18

La Défense, Paris 67
landscape 6, 40–1

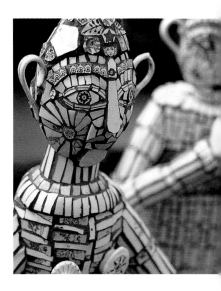

Latin America 15, 38
Levesque, Mireille 18
light 49, 50, 53, 75
    workrooms 145
lighting a mosaic 155
linking spaces 42
living rooms 90, 106, 132

maintenance of mosaics 154
maison Picassiette 68, 69
marble 6, 22–3, 46, 75, 143, 146, 147
marine motifs 36–7
mass-production 16
Matisse, Henri 57
Mayans 15
meshing 144, 149
metallic materials 6, 12, 23, 46, 54,
    60, 61, 120
micromosaic 23, 56, 100
mirror mosaic 26–7, 54, 75, 110–11,
    112–15, 120, 122, 147
mixed media 6, 28–9, 54, 60–1
Mondrian, Piet 42
mood 46, 47

mother-of-pearl 15, 28
Muir, Jane 37
murals 46, 68, 69, 76, 152
Mussi, Cleo 57, 59, 68, 117, 126

Newnham, Rebecca 39, 57, 122, 134
nippers 145, 146, 147

opera 57
opus 57
opus vermiculatum 58

panels 76, 78–9, 142
Parc Güell, Barcelona 16, 17, 55
paths 42, 61, 77, 88–9
patios 46, 70–1
patterns 6, 7, 11, 14, 18, 32, 34–5,
    38–9, 42–3, 49, 55, 56–9, 62, 76, 79,
    80, 92, 93, 122
paving 88–9
pebble mosaics 6, 10, 28, 46, 55, 88,
    122
Picasso, Pablo 32
planning projects 142–3

plant patterns 14, 18, 38–9
pools 42, 55, 80–1, 122, 151, 152
posture 144
pots 120–1, 142, 144
practical considerations 46–7, 48–9,
    72, 143
Prague 17
pre-Columbian art 15
preparing materials 146–7
preparing surfaces 72, 74–5, 148–9
priming 148
PVA (white) glue 150

Raeli, Salvatore 32, 39, 55, 58, 63
Ravenna 18, 40
Reeve, Max 100
Renaissance 29, 32, 42, 82
representational mosaics 11, 32,
    58–9
Riley, Tabby 48, 112–15
Romans, ancient 10–11, 18, 22, 32, 34,
    35, 40, 42, 62
rope patterns 42, 62, 93

safety 145, 146, 147
Saini, Nek Chand 126
Saint Phalle, Niki de 18, 126
salvaged materials 28, 29
scale 46, 47, 72, 90, 122
screens 109
scroll patterns 11, 62
sculpture 7, 126–8, 132–3, 134–5
    sculptural head 129–31
sealing 148, 154
semi-precious stones 15, 28
shapes 56–9
    sculptural 134–5
sheet mosaic 24–5, 146
shells 15, 28–9, 55
Shimizu, Takako 35, 48, 60, 133
silver 23, 38, 54, 55, 122
siting a mosaic 6, 7, 47, 48–9, 143, 155
sitting rooms 90, 106, 132
sketching 56–7, 62, 142
Skinner, Christopher 100
small projects 106–7, 142
smalti 6, 23, 146
smashed ceramics 17, 26, 54, 55,
    60–1, 146
Smith, Stephen 33, 41
snakes and ladders floor 84–7
spirals 14, 42, 58
splashbacks 46, 61, 76

sponging 153
squares 42, 58, 80
stained glass 27, 143
    table 103–5
stars 14, 42
Stewart, Claire 6, 34
still life 40–1
stone mosaics 60, 61, 69, 75, 88–9, 90,
    101, 122, 143
storage 23, 24, 109, 145
stylized designs 14, 38
Sumeria 10
Sun City, South Africa 80
surfaces 72–5, 148–9
surprise elements 54, 55

tables 46, 100–2, 107, 109
    stained glass table 103–5
Tarot Garden, Tuscany 19
terracotta 120, 142, 144, 148
tesserae 10, 23, 24, 42, 46, 55, 60, 90,
    116, 120, 126, 143
texture 54, 60–1
Tiffany, Louis Comfort 17, 52
tiles 24–5, 26–7, 143, 147
tools 145, 146, 147, 155
trellis patterns 76

Victorian age 32, 81
Vienna 17, 67, 103
Vondee, Norma 6, 36, 37, 39, 61, 84,
    110, 127, 134

Wales, Rosalind 41
walls 7, 11, 52, 68–9, 72–5
water features 46, 120, 122–3, 152
water resistance 6, 26, 46, 48, 75, 152
water supply 145
Wharton, Edith 82
Williams, Greg 72
Wilson, Sheryl 117
wood 60, 148
workspaces 144–5

acknowledgements

The publisher and authors would like to thank Christopher Skinner, Martin Cohen and all the mosaic artists that have contributed to the book.

Emma Biggs
Mosaic Workshop
Unit B, 443–449 Holloway Road
London N7 6LJ.
Abstract colour panel (pp. 78–9).

Celia Gregory
Cohen Gregory
2nd Floor, Enterprise House
Tudor Grove, London E9 7QL.
*Stained glass table (pp. 102–5);
Mosaic hearth (pp. 94–7) and
Candle sconce (pp. 136–9).*

Tessa Hunkin
Mosaic Workshop
Unit B, 443–449 Holloway Road
London N7 6LJ.
Sculptural head (pp. 128–31).

Tabby Riley
15 Dumont Road
London N16 0NR.
Mirror mosaic (pp. 112–15).

Norma Vondee
8 Benson Quay
Wapping
London E1 9TR
*Snakes and ladders floor (pp. 84–7);
Uni garden seat (pp. 118–19).*

The publisher would like to thank the photographer Polly Eltes and the following individuals, designers and companies for assisting with photography and for allowing us to photograph their mosaics.

Amanda and Gareth; Anna Tabata Cominitti (ACT); Ann Hughes at Mosaik; Bishop Challoner School; Christopher Skinner; Claire Stewart; Cleo Mussi; Elizabeth De'Ath; Elaine M.Goodwin; Fired Earth; Flower Store; Robert Grace: Director of the Gallery of Mosaic Art and Design, Suite 324, Business Design Centre, 52 Upper Street, London N1 0QH; Jane Muir; Jenni Pretor-Pinney: Yoga Place, Bethnal Green, London; John Freeman; Lauren Lorenzo; Marion Lynch: Interior Designer; Martin Cheek; Martin Cohen; Mrs Lewis; Norma Vondee; Paris Ceramics; Peter Bibby; Rebecca Newnham; Rollo Armstrong; Rosalind Wates; Salvatore Raeli; Stephen Charnock; Stephen Smith: Mozaiek Art; Takako Shimizu; Tony Bruce; Trevor Caley.

picture credits

t = top b = bottom c = centre
l = left r = right

Adrian Taylor p. 106bl.
AKG Photo London p. 12.
Ancient Art and Architecture Collection Ltd p. 10br.
Bridgeman Art Library p. 15bl, 17br.
British Museum p. 15tl ©The British Museum.
Caroline Arber p. 107tr.
Celia Gregory pp. 70b, 82bl, 100tr.

Corbis Images
  pp. 11© Morton Beebe, S.F
  13 © Mimmo Jodice
  14b © Hanan Isachar
  16 © Charles & Josette Lenars,
  18 bl © Massimo Listri,
  35t © Jonathon Blair,
  67t © Stephanie Colasanti,
  69t © Art on File,
  82br © Audrey Gibson,
  133bl © Charles & Josette Lenars.
DebiTreloar pp. 38r, 55tl, 93br, 107br, 108bl, 109tr.
Edifice p. 40 bl, 41br, 55t.
Elizabeth Whiting Associates pp. 63tr, 76br, 80.
Fired Earth pp. 46bl, 75, 92br.
Garden Picture Library
  pp. 70t © Liz Macmurdie.
  88bl, br © John Glover.
Jane Muir p. 37t.
Jonathan Buckley p. 42bl.
Jo Whitworth pp. 88bc, 89.
Maggy Howarth p. 35br.
Mainstream p. 73 © Ray Main,
  p.93t © Ray Main/Jonas/W5.
Martin Cheek pp. 33l, 37br, 133t.
Paris Ceramics pp. 62, 90.
Peter Andersen p. 83, at Chelsea Flower Show 2001, *A Garden for Learning* designed by Woodford West; p.88br, at Chelsea Flower Show 2001, garden designed by Bunny Guinness.
Rosalind Wates p. 41tr.
Sarah Cuttle pp. 26, 42br, 49tr, 134bl.
Spike Powell pp. 29br, 69br, 92bl, 101tl.
Stephen Smith p. 33tr, 41l.
Tim Imrie pp. 68br, 107tl, 116bl, 121tl.
Trip pp. 10l, 14t, 67b © H. Rogers. 17tl © C. Gibson. 66 © J. Isachsen.

left *Masks*: a skilful and intricate mosaic of dramatic masks by Salvatore Raeli.